CALLED TO BE FREE

Called To Be Free

Reflections on the Meaning of
Christian Freedom

George A. Maloney, SJ

ALBA·HOUSE   NEW·YORK

SOCIETY OF ST. PAUL, 2187 VICTORY BLVD., STATEN ISLAND, NEW YORK 10314

ST PAULS

Library of Congress Cataloging-in-Publication Data

Maloney, George A., 1924-
    Called to be free: reflections on the meaning of Christian freedom / George A.
Maloney.
        p. cm.
    Includes bibliographical references.
    ISBN 0-8189-0837-8
    1. Freedom (Theology) 2. Liberty — Religious aspects — Christianity. I. Title.

BT810.2.M34 2000
261.7'2 — dc21

                                                                              00-035535

Imprimi Potest:
Rev. Edward Mathie, SJ
Provincial of the Wisconsin Province
November 10, 1999

Produced and designed in the United States of America by the
Fathers and Brothers of the Society of St. Paul,
2187 Victory Boulevard, Staten Island, New York 10314-6603,
as part of their communications apostolate.

ISBN: 0-8189-0837-8

Printing Information:

Current Printing - first digit   1   2   3   4   5   6   7   8   9   10

Year of Current Printing - first year shown

2001   2002   2003   2004   2005   2006   2007   2008   2009   2010

Dedication

To Reverend Bernard Wolfe:
A humble child of God and a priest of Christ forever,
who helps the Lord to set captives free
in all his various priestly works.

Table of Contents

Introduction

God's awesome gift of himself through his Son Jesus in his Spirit comes to us in his gifts of freedom and infinite love. In his pursuit of our response, he also gives us the frightening power to say *yes* or *no* to his gifts, to accept or reject them. We find ourselves tempted, as Jesus was in the desert, to bow in loving surrender to our eternal Father's majesty and tender love or to turn away into the darkness of self-centered and ultimately self-destructive concerns.

One of the most penetrating of modern authors ever to grapple with this mystery of human freedom is the Russian novelist, Feodor Dostoevsky. In his legend of the Grand Inquisitor — told by Ivan the "atheist," to his brother, the novice monk Alyosha, in the novel *The Brothers Karamazov* — Dostoevsky tells us of the return of Jesus to this earth. This time Jesus appears in Seville, Spain of the sixteenth century, the time of the *Inquisition*.

After performing a few miracles and arousing the enthusiasm of the crowd — who began clamoring to make him king as the people of old in Palestine did — Jesus is apprehended by order of the ninety-year-old Dominican Cardinal and Grand Inquisitor and is thrown into the dungeon. The Grand Inquisitor quizzes Jesus, asking him why he ever came back. The freedom he came on earth to give us was too much of a responsibility for human beings to handle. The Inquisitor accuses Jesus:

I tell you that man is tormented by no greater anxiety
than to find someone quickly to whom he can hand over
that gift of freedom with which the ill-fated creature is
born. But only one who can appease their conscience can
take over their freedom.... Instead of taking human
freedom from them, you made it greater than ever! Did
you forget that man prefers peace, and even death, to
freedom of choice in the knowledge of good and evil?
Nothing is more seductive for man than his freedom of
conscience, but nothing is a greater cause of his
suffering.... Instead of taking possession of men's
freedom you increased it, and burdened the spiritual
kingdom of mankind with suffering forever. You desired
man's free love, that he should follow you freely, enticed
and taken captive by you. In place of the rigid ancient
law, man must hereafter with free heart decide for
himself what is good and what is evil, having only your
image before him as his guide. But did you not know
that he would in the end reject even your image and your
truth if he is weighed down with the fearful burden of
free choice?[1]

We Are More Slaves Than Freed Persons

You and I are more slaves than freed persons. Part of our
slavery consists in having forgotten what true freedom — the
freedom of the children of God — means. We often are content to
live in the narrow confines of our slavery, mainly because
everyone else is in the same prison. Blindness would not be so
great a suffering if everyone were blind and never knew the
possibility of sight. But blindness would become unbearable if
there were among all blind persons one who could really see!

The way we perceive ourselves, God, and the world is fairly
much the same way others perceive them. That, precisely, is part
of our slavery. But Jesus Christ came among us with the eyes of

God. He was "…the true light that enlightens all men" (Jn 1:9).
That light shines in our darkness and cannot be overpowered by
it (Jn 1:5).

Jesus Descends into Hades

The famous Byzantine icon of Jesus' *Descent into Hades*
authoritatively illustrates the power of Jesus Christ to set us
free. This is the icon that is typically reverenced in the Christian
East from the vigil of Christ's resurrection from the dead until
the Church celebrates his *Ascension* into glory. Since the actual
event of Christ's resurrection from the dead was not witnessed
by any human being, the artist chose to portray the mystery of
his resurrection by depicting his descent into Hades to free
those there by pulling them up out of the underworld.

In this icon the risen Savior is pictured as the "New
Adam" lifting up those in Hades to share in God's own divine
life (2 P 1:4). J. Breck well describes the power of the risen Jesus
in this icon: "The Paschal icon thus proclaims to the eyes of
faith that life itself has penetrated into the realm of death to
perform a new act of creation: a transformation of the old Adam
into a perfect likeness of the new Man, the glorified Son of
God."[2]

In this icon we see Jesus drawing Adam and Eve out of the
abyss into a new life bathed in the light of Christ. Christ
becomes the archetype of our restoration to the fullness of life
bringing us the hope that we too can attain the wholeness that
once was ours when we were created in God's image and
likeness (Gn 1:26-27). Jesus Christ, the God-Man, is the perfect
image of God. If we have lost our freedom, Christ, the icon of
our salvation, brings us the hope of attaining wholeness once
again.[3] This process of being freed by the risen Christ is the core
message of this book.

Where There Is the Spirit, There Is Liberty

This book deals with the power of the Spirit of the risen Lord to set us free. This freedom is conceived in the New Testament as a gift that we receive when we seek to place Jesus Christ, God's Logos or Word, at the center of our lives. The Christian freedom that Jesus came to give us consists in a spiritual revolution of the mind as St. Paul wrote:

> Your mind must be renewed by a spiritual revolution
> so that you can put on the new self that has been
> created in God's way in the goodness and holiness of
> the truth (Eph 4:23-24).

Jesus spoke only occasionally of his ability to set us free. Yet his work during his lifetime on earth and now through his glorious resurrection is precisely to set us free! He preached the coming of the Kingdom of God and he promised to send us his Spirit who would lead us into all truth: "If you make my word your home," he told us, "you will be my disciples; you will learn the truth and the truth will make you free" (Jn 8:31-32). Yet rarely beyond these words does Jesus speak formally of freedom.

St. Paul Teaches Us Christian Freedom

It is St. Paul who speaks often about the freeing power of the Spirit of Jesus. This Spirit dwells within us who are Christians, making our very own bodies temples of the indwelling Trinity (1 Cor 3:16; 1 Cor 6:19). He brings us into direct contact with the risen Jesus who, along with the heavenly Father, dwells within us (Jn 14:23). He is a life-giving Spirit, making us truly children of God (Rm 8:15; Gal 4:6). The love of God abounds in our hearts through the Holy Spirit given to us (Rm 5:5).

We change our perception of the world around us as we are

set free from the illusions of the "world" (Eph 4:17). We are no longer bound by our own desires to control reality, to fashion it according to our own whims and passions. We let go of our defenses. Freedom in the Spirit allows us to walk in the gentleness of children of God who seek at all times to please the heavenly Father just as Jesus, the freest of all human beings, did in his earthly life.

The freedom presented in this book is freedom on a spiritual level, a freedom that allows us through deeper prayer to turn progressively to God living within us as at our center. Such a freedom results in the attainment of wholeness, of integration, and it enables us to actuate, by God's creative, loving grace, the potential he has locked within our being. At a time in history when psychology has become the main source of reference telling us who we are, who is normal and who is not, a theological anthropology is needed to provide us with a framework in which we can understand ourselves and the true and ultimate meaning of our human freedom.

Freedom through Contemplation

God's healing love comes to us in prayer as we let go of our own agendas and enter into deep contemplation, letting his presence be experienced by us in the Holy Spirit (Rm 8:26-27). With love we open ourselves to the Spirit's gifts of love and freedom. In a way this book is indirectly a book about deeper contemplation. It seeks to show how contemplation is ultimately a growing experience of God's infinite love within us and around us throughout the entire universe, making us true children of God, new creatures in the Lord (2 Cor 5:17). As we experience this great love, our lives change because the perceptions of ourselves and of God and of the world change.

In contemplation, God's Spirit is free to communicate with

us the indwelling Trinity, directly, without words or images of our own choosing and to the degree that we have purified our hearts of all self-centeredness. Like Lazarus we are always coming forth from the darkness of our dead selves into the light of Christ's presence. We discover in adoring that loving presence throughout the day, in the context of each moment and of each event, that freedom is ultimately gained when we act as free persons in Christ.

Jesus embraced each moment of his earthly life with maximum freedom. He took his life and gave it back joyfully to his heavenly Father as gift for gift received. So likewise, we Christians must live freely by taking our lives into our own hands, determining each thought, word and deed according to what would most please our heavenly Father.

These pages are not offered as a definitive work on the philosophy of freedom. It is a gathering of personal insights on freedom that the author has culled from studying and praying through Holy Scripture, especially in the Johannine and Pauline writings, and the early Eastern Fathers along with the writings of the great mystics of the Church. This work is humbly offered to the reader in the hope that she or he will be helped in the greatest work of one's life: to become free in the Spirit of Jesus so as to live consciously in the love of God, bringing forth the fruits of the Holy Spirit: love, joy, peace, patience, kindness, generosity, faithfulness, gentleness and self control (Gal 5:22).

If you, the reader, will become a bit freer through the reading of this book, the author also will share in that freedom which is always gauged by greater love and humble service to all, who seek to be set free!

George A. Maloney, SJ
November 21, 2000
The Presentation of Mary in the Temple

Biblical Abbreviations

OLD TESTAMENT

Genesis	Gn	Nehemiah	Ne	Baruch	Ba
Exodus	Ex	Tobit	Tb	Ezekiel	Ezk
Leviticus	Lv	Judith	Jdt	Daniel	Dn
Numbers	Nb	Esther	Est	Hosea	Ho
Deuteronomy	Dt	1 Maccabees	1 M	Joel	Jl
Joshua	Jos	2 Maccabees	2 M	Amos	Am
Judges	Jg	Job	Jb	Obadiah	Ob
Ruth	Rt	Psalms	Ps	Jonah	Jon
1 Samuel	1 S	Proverbs	Pr	Micah	Mi
2 Samuel	2 S	Ecclesiastes	Ec	Nahum	Na
1 Kings	1 K	Song of Songs	Sg	Habakkuk	Hab
2 Kings	2 K	Wisdom	Ws	Zephaniah	Zp
1 Chronicles	1 Ch	Sirach	Si	Haggai	Hg
2 Chronicles	2 Ch	Isaiah	Is	Malachi	Ml
Ezra	Ezr	Jeremiah	Jr	Zechariah	Zc
		Lamentations	Lm		

NEW TESTAMENT

Matthew	Mt	Ephesians	Eph	Hebrews	Heb
Mark	Mk	Philippians	Ph	James	Jm
Luke	Lk	Colossians	Col	1 Peter	1 P
John	Jn	1 Thessalonians	1 Th	2 Peter	2 P
Acts	Ac	2 Thessalonians	2 Th	1 John	1 Jn
Romans	Rm	1 Timothy	1 Tm	2 John	2 Jn
1 Corinthians	1 Cor	2 Timothy	2 Tm	3 John	3 Jn
2 Corinthians	2 Cor	Titus	Tt	Jude	Jude
Galatians	Gal	Philemon	Phm	Revelation	Rv

CALLED TO BE FREE

Chapter One

God's Freedom

Today we are seeing the Holy Spirit of the risen Lord working powerfully in the hearts of millions of people of many nations, especially in Eastern Europe, Asia, Central and South America and in Africa. A treasured fire burns powerfully in their hearts for greater freedom to live a fully human life in dignity, befitting God's human children.

Gustavo Gutierrez-Merino, one of the leading theologians to articulate "liberation theology," expresses this aspiration for liberation:

> A broad and deep aspiration for liberation inflames the history of mankind in our day, liberation from all that limits or keeps man from self-fulfillment, liberation from all impediment to the exercise of his freedom.[1]

We are seeing a general sense of liberation on social, economic and religious levels spreading over the world.

What Is Freedom?

Authentic freedom and authentic love are two concepts that are used universally around the world in our modern times

1

and yet are described and understood in so many contradictory ways. Philosophers would offer us all sorts of definitions of freedom.

> Freedom in general is the state of not being forced or determined by something external, insofar as it is joined to a definite internal faculty of self-determination. Different kinds of freedom are distinguished according to the kinds of pressures which are excluded.[2]

Mortimer J. Adler describes human freedom in these terms:
Freedom: A man who is able
  (a) under favorable circumstances, to act as he wishes for his own individual good as he sees it
  (b) through acquired virtue or wisdom to will or live as he ought in conformity to the moral law or an ideal befitting human nature, or
  (c) by a power inherent in human nature, to change his own character creatively by deciding for himself what he shall do or shall become is free in the sense that he has in himself the ability or power whereby he can make what he does his own action and what he achieves his property.[3]

Socio-biologists like Edward Wilson of Harvard would place our human freedom in our ability to perform for the group, the colony, in much the way that insects, birds and animals are free to live for the community. In the freedom of B.F. Skinner, man now controls his own destiny because he knows what must be done and can now know how to do it. But this would rule out any *metanoia* on our part and would deny any gift of freedom from God. E. Marcuse's one-dimensional human person puts all liberation within the power of each person.

Political activists would put all human freedom in
liberation from social, political and economic oppression, but
such liberation theology forgets that unless we human persons
are spiritually freed, we will always carry our own
imprisonment where we go.

Born To Be Free and Loving

All human beings the world over seek freedom; more
basically they seek love as the key to their desperate search for
meaningful and lasting happiness. We seek love. We also seek
freedom to become the true, unique, beautiful self that God
from all eternity has chosen us in Christ Jesus to be that we
might share in his eternal life (Eph 1:4).

Love and freedom are not identical, but each needs the
other as its complement. God, who is love (1 Jn 4:8), is also the
perfection of freedom. We cannot comprehend what true love
and freedom mean in our lives unless we understand how God
is both love and freedom by nature. The spark of love and
freedom that emanates from the flaming heart of God can be
known only from its Source.

We are created freely by God in his own image and
likeness to share his love and freedom in our earthly existence
as well as in the future, eternal life. The three Persons of the
Trinity, a community of loving, free Persons, in a burst of
creative freedom, "other" themselves in the otherness of
creation. God freely wishes us to collaborate with him in our
self-creation and self-transcendence. In doing so, we work
along with God's own love, the Holy Spirit. Freedom of the
Spirit is of the essence of God's nature as is love.

True freedom can never be properly understood except in
the context of love. Theologians and philosophers might ask
the question: "Is God free because he loves, or is he love

because he is free?" With these two words, love and freedom, we touch something very basic in the awesome mystery of the Trinity. Our puny words fail us and it is in profound and silent adoration that we stand before God, to search within the Trinity to discover what authentic love and genuine freedom really mean.

It is only in the revelation that Jesus has made as God-Man in the New Testament that we are able to know something of the existence and nature of the three related Persons of Father, Son and Holy Spirit, united in one divine nature. Perfect love and freedom are salient characteristics of that nature. It is this perfect and free love that the Triune Persons share with us (2 P 1:4).

An Apophatic Understanding of the Trinity

But is it possible for us to plunge into the depths of the inner, infinite nature of God and come to some understanding of God's essence as love in freedom?

The early Eastern mystics — for example, St. Basil, St. Gregory of Nyssa and St. Gregory Nazianzen of the 4th century — in their defense against heresies that denied God was a Trinity, three unique Persons in one divine nature, would answer in the affirmative. Their approach in writing of the mystery of the Trinity was of an *apophatic* nature. *Apophatic* is usually thought of as a "negative" approach, an approach which denies that rational knowledge is the only knowledge we can have about God. Actually, however, the apophatic approach is much more than that. It opens us up to a "positive" experiential knowledge of God. This is an infused knowledge given by God to those who are "pure of heart." Through it they "see" or "experience" God in the "luminous darkness" of faith, hope and love.[4]

God, A "No-Being"

St. John Damascene has this to say about the infinite and incomprehensible nature of God:

> God is infinite and incomprehensible and all that is comprehensible about him is his infinity and incomprehensibility.... God does not belong to a class of existing things. He receives no existence, but is above all existing things. If all forms of knowledge have to do with what exists, that which is above knowledge must be above all (created) essence, and what is above essence must be above human knowledge.[5]

Nicholas Berdyaev, the Russian philosopher and theologian (1874-1948), grounded in the apophatic language of the Orthodox mystics of the Christian East, describes through the symbol or myth he calls the *meon* (from the Greek: *to men on,* meaning, "no-being") how God is eternal, loving and free prior to any being.[6] Freedom, for Berdyaev, must not be a "thing" created by God, but must exist in God. Both the mystery of God and the mystery of freedom and love in God cannot be fully grasped by rational concepts which derive from the world of created beings.

He writes in *Dream and Reality* that the mystery of freedom is not susceptible of any rationalizations:

> The issues involved in this problem have led me to the recognition of uncreated and uncaused freedom, which is tantamount to the recognition of an irreducible mystery, admitting of intuitive description but not of definition.[7]

Freedom through the revelation of Jesus Christ can ultimately exist only in God as an essential characteristic of God's nature as love. There is no human freedom without God as its Source.[8]

The Godhead: The Eternal Source of All

Gregory Nazianzen, the great 4th century Greek theologian, who wrote so lyrically about the Trinity, describes the eternal God as the Source and Goal of diversity through personal relationships within the Trinity:

> The nature is one in three; it is God; but that which makes the unity is the Father, from whom and to whom the order of person runs its course, not in such a way that the nature is confused, but that it is possessed without distinction of time or of will or of power.[9]

The Eastern Fathers of the early centuries of the Church, in writing about the mystery of the Trinity, did not begin with God the Father as the ultimate Source. *Godhead* is the term they used to describe the incomprehensible, the ineffable, the "unmanifested" or "undifferentiated" dimension of God's essence or nature. In the words of Pseudo-Dionysius,[10] "In the Godhead is the fullness of being, the Silence out of which will come relational communication within the Trinity and toward us human beings."

In the stillness of eternity, the Godhead moves from silence to speech (the Word), from perfect repose and motionlessness to sharing itself (the Father) in perfect freedom and love (the Spirit). Because of the Godhead's fullness and infinite richness, it cannot be classified in a quantified way or in categories like beings that receive their existence from a higher origin. The

Godhead is beyond all being and yet is found in all beings, including ourselves. It tremulously holds us and the whole world in its grasp. God is not an "object" to whom we go in prayer to communicate and to receive "things."

The Tri-Unity of God

The Godhead would remain forever the Void of infinite potentialities had it not chosen to freely express itself in a triune fashion. The Father is the Godhead as Mystery seeking understanding,[11] the Word is the Godhead's Expression of this Mystery, and the Spirit is the love engendered by this Mystery and its Expression.

Gabriel Marcel, the French Catholic philosopher, poet and playwright, enunciates an important principle in inter-personal relationships that applies initially to God as Trinity. "The *I* is the child of the *WE*."[12] There are three elements in the love relationship between the Persons of the Trinity. The first of these is *availability*. The Lover must freely will to be totally available to the one loved. The second element is *mutuality*, the reciprocal will to share one's total being with the beloved and vice-versa. The third characteristic of intimate love is *self-emptying*, freely given.

The eternal Mind of the Godhead has a thought which begets a Word that perfectly mirrors the Father (my "Abba") which gave birth to it. The Spirit of reciprocal love thus engendered is the Holy Spirit who binds the Mind with the Word and imparts to each something of its own uniqueness. The *I* is truly the child of the *WE* in this Trinitarian community.

In our discussion, we must be careful not to project our earthly concept of time into our understanding of occurrences taking place from all eternity, actions that never knew a beginning or/and will never know an end but always "are." St. Gregory Nazianzen says that the Son and the Holy Spirit, though they proceed from the Father (each in a different way), are "co-everlasting" as he is. The linking of the generation of the Son or the procession of the Spirit with any idea of time is improper, "for those things which are the origin of time cannot be subject to time."[13]

Ecstasy

The Source pours the fullness of his divinity into his Son (Col 2:9). What we could never know by our own knowledge, God's Word has revealed to us. God is a community, a family of loving persons who freely empty themselves in order to express their unity and also their unique *I-ness* in ecstatic love.

Some Greek Fathers, among them Pseudo-Dionysius and St. Maximus the Confessor, were fond of describing God's love within the Trinity as *ecstasy*. By their use of the Greek word *ekstasis* they were referring to a movement out of the self toward another in self-emptying love, an habitual "standing outside" of one's controlled and self-possessed being, the burning, driving force of the Holy Spirit, the gift of Love toward some one Other. It is a coming home and a finding of one's identity as a unique person in the loving surrender to another. The Father in ecstasy empties himself into his Son through his Spirit of love. Such self-emptying is returned from the Son to the Father through the bonding Spirit.

The Bonding Love of the Holy Spirit

This inter-relationship between the Father and Son in self-knowledge through the self-surrendering gift of each one to the other is made possible through the Holy Spirit who is the gift of Love and Freedom between the Father and Son. This is why there is always a triple movement within the one

Godhead. It is the Holy Spirit, who eternally illumines the mystery of the intimate love of Father and Son. And if the Father and Son mutually know and affirm themselves, this, too, is necessarily brought about by the Holy Spirit who enables them, not only mutually to affirm themselves as Father and Son, but mutually to recognize themselves as such.

The Holy Spirit, thus, cannot be an accidental, created relation or something produced. In a mysterious manner the Holy Spirit unites the Father and the Son eternally in love. The Spirit makes it possible that the unity of the Trinity can still be shared without destroying the unity in the diversity of persons, who equally share in the one divine essence.

We can see, therefore, that the ineffable mystery of the Trinity, which escapes our own human comprehension, can, however, be known and experienced in and through Jesus Christ and the Holy Spirit. God has not only determined to reveal the truth of this mystery to us, but in that revelation has made the mystery of the Trinity the beginning and end of all reality, of all love and freedom. God effects our fulfillment precisely in and through the activities of the triune God in the context of the history of our salvation.

Let us turn now to a consideration of how the Trinity's love and freedom directly impact our eternal destiny. St. Paul in his letter to the Ephesians succinctly speaks of our predestination in God, now and in the eternal life to come:

> Before the world was made, he chose us, chose us in
> Christ, to be holy and spotless, and to live through
> love in his presence... to make us praise the glory of
> his grace, his free gift to us in the Beloved, in
> whom... we gain our freedom, the forgiveness of our
> sins (Eph 1:4-7).

Chapter Two

Called To Be Free

A modern French contemplative and social activist who worked among the poor and alienated of Parisian society, Madeleine Delbrel, wrote: "God weighs more than all the world put together."[1] The writer was not pitting God against the world and encouraging us to choose him over all his creatures. She was rather giving voice to contemporary women and men in their desperate, and in some ways pathetic, longing for perfect *Beauty*. It is this desire that gnaws at the center of our being for the *Unpossessable* that makes all other possessions vain, as the poet Francis Thompson wrote in *The Hound of Heaven*.

God alone is great, beautiful, powerful, all loving and completely free. In this chapter let us explore God's eternal call to each and every human person to be a unique manifestation of his love and freedom. Let us try to find an answer to the question: Who are you, who am I, in God's eternal predestination in and through his Word: Jesus Christ?

Modern Images of the Human Person

Great writers and philosophers through the ages have fashioned for us a *pantheon* of human models to help us answer this question of our true identity. The tabloids, novels, TV

11

programs, movies, songs and advertisements have also fashioned
a great variety of images of who we should be. But sadly enough
such images all too often highlight our self-centeredness and
confusion which only stifle God's answer as to why he has
created us.

The Psalmist describes the beauty and nobility to which
we are called according to God's plan:

> Ah, what is man that you should spare a thought for
> him, the son of man that you should care for him? Yet
> you have made him little less than a god, you have
> crowned him with glory and splendor, made him lord
> over the work of your hands, set all things under his
> feet. (Ps 8:5-7)

Made in the Image of God

The early Fathers of the Church, in asking the question
concerning the nature of human beings, turned to God and his
divinely inspired word for the answer. "And God said, 'Let us
make man according to our image and likeness...' male and
female he made them" (Gn 1:26-27).

They interpreted this text as indicating by divine
inspiration a special creative act on the part of God which set
human beings on a plane completely different from the rest of
creation. Michelangelo, in his famous painting in the Sistine
Chapel, pictured God as reaching out and touching Adam,
allowing something of his very life to flow into him. God creates
human beings, not as he does other things, which are already
complete in their relationship of dependence upon God. Only
human beings are created as *unfinished* beings, who in their first
moments of existence immediately enter into a relationship to
God of persons to persons. Not only are Adam and Eve created

freely by God through his communicative Word, but they are created in God and for God. Human beings are to find their fullness in God as *Other*.

The Uniqueness of Human Persons

Sergius Bulgakov, the Russian theologian, described Adam's uniqueness over all other creatures as consisting in his having been made by God to be a self-positing creature.[1] The image of God in us consists ultimately in our possessing the spiritual faculties of intellect and will through which instruments we may posit ourselves as an *I*, dependent on the Absolute *I* of God.

The early Eastern Fathers interpreted the Genesis story of the free and independent creation by God of human beings in the image and likeness of God to mean that our total personhood finds its full meaning in the Prime Image of God. This refers to the Logos, the Divine Word, who mirrors as the Speech of God the incomprehensible Mind of God. God in absolute transcendence creates us, not as totally independent beings, but precisely as self-positing beings, able, in freedom and love, to grow through obedience into an ever more perfect image and likeness of our Prototype, the Divine Word.

Jesus is the perfect Image of God (Col 1:15). We are created according to his likeness. We are not the perfect image of God, but in our very being we grow into that likeness through a personal relationship to God in and through Jesus Christ. Emil Brunner beautifully describes our ontological relationship to God through the Word thus:

God creates man in such a way that in this very creation man is summoned to receive the Word actively, that is, he is called to listen, to understand,

and to believe. God creates man's being in such a way
that man knows that he is determined and conditioned
by God, and in this fact is truly human.

The being of man as an *I* is being from and in the
Divine *Thou,* or more exactly, from and in the Divine
Word, whose claim "calls" man's being into
existence.... The characteristic imprint of man,
however, only develops on the basis of Divine
determination, as an answer to a call, by means of a
decision. The necessity for decision, an obligation
which he can never evade, is the distinguishing feature
of man... it is the being created by God to stand "over-
against" him, who can reply to God, and who in this
answer alone fulfills — or destroys — the purpose of
God's creation.[2]

Freely Chosen in Jesus Christ

Whenever St. Paul writes about God's free election of us to
share in the Trinity's inner life, he links that choice to Jesus
Christ:

Before the world was made, he chose us, chose us in
Christ, to be holy and spotless, and to live through love
in his presence, determining that we should become his
adopted children, through Jesus Christ. (Eph 1:4-5)

God has given us the grace to know the mystery of his
eternal purpose in creating us. This is the hidden plan he made in
Christ from the beginning (Eph 1:9). Jesus is the purpose behind
God's every word and will. Karl Barth, the Swiss theologian,
states how Jesus is the goal and fulfillment of God's eternal will.
"Whatever comes to man in the freedom of God and in the

fulfillment of his eternal will comes first of all to Jesus as *the* elected man. When God elects Jesus, he elects, not only an eternal will (Jesus as the electing God), but also a temporal fact (Jesus as the elected man)."[3]

This is surely Paul's understanding of our eternal salvation in and through Christ when he writes: "Before anything was created, he existed, and he holds all things together in himself" (Col 1:17).[4] We can believe, therefore, that Jesus is, and always has been, the one mediator between God and ourselves. Eternally chosen through God's free will, Jesus teaches us the truth about God, a truth that will set us free. Jesus said in his public life: "If you make my word your home you will indeed be my disciples, and you will learn the truth and the truth will make you free" (Jn 8:31-32). Christ is the Way, the Truth and the Life (Jn 14:6).

A Graceful Love

Love, in order to exist, in God or human beings, must always be loving, always freely pouring itself out from its own abundance, always giving of itself. Tied to the mysterious makeup of God as an *I* that is also a *WE*, is God's bursting forth from within the Trinity's own perfect, circular, loving, self-contained freedom to love us so that we might share in the freedom of the eternal Word, Jesus Christ, by accepting that divine life. The nature of God is such that, while being in the Trinity is one in essence, this demands a plurality as objects of his love, of his infinite self-giving in perfect freedom.

The first and necessary truth about God's freedom that he wishes to share with us, made according to his own image and likeness which is Jesus Christ, is that God's nature or essence is absolute transcendence. This means that God, before his free decision to create creatures, angels and human beings and all

other material creatures, can never be dependent upon them.
While creatures are completely dependent upon the eternal
Creator for their existence, God is always transcendent in his
perfections. God can never be coerced to create.

It is the early Eastern Christian mystical writers, especially
the Greek Fathers, who carefully distinguished between the
essence of God that is one nature, equally shared by the three
Divine Persons, and God's one nature in the multiplied world of
creation. Pseudo-Dionysius of the 5th century described the
movement outwardly toward the created world as a "going
forth" of God *(proodos* in Greek). The importance of this
distinction is rooted in God's revelation. His essence no human
being can visibly see or intellectually comprehend with the
human mind. No angel or human person has ever seen God and
lived (Ex 33:23; 1 Jn 4:12; Jn 1:18; 6:46).

Sharing God's Nature

Yet the Good News that Jesus incarnate has made possible
through his Holy Spirit is that God freely and lovingly wishes to
share his very own being with us:

> In making these gifts, he has given us the guarantee of
> something very great and wonderful to come; through
> them you will be able to share the divine nature... (2
> P 1:4)

God only asks of us that we open ourselves to God's many
"goings-forth" in which God wishes to communicate his great,
personalized love to all of his human beings destined to be
eternally in Christ Jesus God's very own children. "Think of the
love that the Father has lavished on us, by letting us be called
God's children; and that is what we are" (1 Jn 3:1).

In our continued response to God's invitation to partake of God's freedom and love consists all our greatness and fulfillment. If we consent by humbling ourselves to our true essence as a creature before our Creator, if we make ourselves supple and malleable in the hands of the Divine Artist, God can make of us his masterpiece.

God *ex nihilo* freely creates this universe and all other material non-human creatures and gives them to us only in order that in and through these gifts we human beings may reach a communion with God and share intimately in the freedom and love of the Trinity.

How does God wish to accomplish this sharing in his transcendent freedom and love? In the Book of Genesis we read two different accounts of the creation of the first man and woman. In Gn 1:26, *man* is a generic term, standing for both man and woman, male and female. God has made all of us according to his own image and likeness. Nothing is hinted at as to our origin or of how our body was formed. Man is found in a world teeming with plants, birds, fish and animals and God commands him to fill the earth and subdue it. Both male and female are included in the commission to go forth in creative work to dominate the world around them and from which they differ by reason of their having been made in the image and likeness of a God who is powerful and creative.

In the second account of Adam and Eve (Gn 2:7,15,18, 21-23), however, we see that Adam is first created out of the earth. He is a part of the material world and lives in the Garden of Eden. God gives him a charge, not to subdue and dominate, control and possess, but to tend and care for the garden with love and concern. But God sees that Adam is lonely. God freely decides to create for him a companion, one who can share intimately with Adam a life, ideas, ideals, concerns, but, above all, in intimate love to share herself in free self-giving and to bring forth new human life through such unifying love. God is reflected now to them, not as a doing God, but as an intimate, self-giving God, who is experienced in the intimacy of the human love of two persons for each other. "No one has ever seen God; but as long as we love one another, God will live in us and his love will be complete in us" (1 Jn 4:12).

Our call to live in intimacy with each other comes out of God's very own nature as a community in loving, self-giving relationships with each member of the triune community to which love brings about a oneness in nature and distinction in person. The mystery of the Trinity has been revealed to us through Jesus Christ in Holy Scripture. This was the work of the eternal Word made flesh that we might know the Father through seeing him imaged in his Son (Jn 14:9; Col 1:15).

God's Uncreated Energies of Love

The history of the development of Christian theology shows us that the primary question of theologians has always been posed as: "If God is ineffable and incomprehensible to us human beings in his absolute transcendence, how does God Trinity fulfill his plan of salvation? If God has created us human beings in the image and likeness of Christ Jesus, how does God share his very own being as Love and Freedom?"

St. Thomas Aquinas, using Aristotle's categories, declares that fallen, human nature through original and personal sins needs a created grace called "sanctifying grace." He writes: "Man needs a power added to his natural power by grace."[5] This he calls "grace," a created thing which God bestows upon our human nature. Habitual grace justifies the soul or makes it acceptable to God. It is the infused, God-assisted habit of doing what God approves. Actual grace is the supernatural reality which God gives us as a means of assistance.

Karl Rahner warns against thinking of grace "materialistically." Grace, he writes, is not a "created sanctifying 'quality' produced in a recipient in a merely causal way by God."[6] Rahner comes very close to describing the "uncreated energies" as grace in terms similar to the Greek Fathers when he writes:

> Each one of the three divine persons communicates himself to man in gratuitous grace in his own personal particularity and diversity. This trinitarian communication is the ontological ground of man's life in grace and eventually of the direct vision of the divine persons in eternity.[7]

God's Holiness

Whenever we read in the Bible that God is holy, we find that it is in the context of God as perfectly good and beautiful and loving. Not needing us human beings, he is still found freely drawing near to us, inviting us to accept his covenantal love. In this covenant he offers to make us free and holy if we but open ourselves up to his outpouring love and the free gift of himself. Having freely created the entire cosmos, God intends to bring everything in it into harmony and beauty, reflecting, darkly as in a mirror, something of his infinite power and beauty, for he is omnipotent, omnipresent and omniscient.

God's Hesed Covenant

In *Genesis* we read how the first man and woman accepted God's communication of himself to them through his Word. He would progressively give himself to them as he gives himself within the Trinity to his own Word. We see God

walking with the proto-parents of us all. He dialogues with
them in the cool of the day; a picture of peace and tranquility
(Gn 2:8, 15). But before that familiarity could flower into a
community of shared life, sin entered.

God's Word, spoken by God in the human heart and
listened to by Adam and Eve in loving acceptance, was rejected
by the thrust to take God's gift of freedom and turn it into a
false, enslaving independence. The early Greek Fathers
distinguished between two types of freedom. The first they
called *autexousion* or self-possession. This is the God-given
power bestowed on us when we were created according to
God's own image and likeness. We as human beings will
always possess this freedom, even when we sin as did Adam
and Eve. This we all experience. It is the ability to determine
our choices as autonomous agents always intrinsically
empowered to be the masters of our own destiny.

The second freedom they called *eleutheria*. Heinrich
Schlier writes: "More concretely the New Testament uses
eleutheria for freedom from sin (e.g., Rm 6:18-23; Jn 8:31-36)
and from the Law (Rm 7:2; Gal 2:4) and from death (Rm 6:21).
Freedom is freedom from an existence which in sin leads
through the Law to death."[8] Such freedom involves living
according to our fully integrated human nature. It is the entire
human person living according to his or her total nature in the
process of growing into total fulfillment as one lives in Christ
Jesus.

The Effects of Human Sin

This is true freedom under the new law of love (Gal 5:13).
"When Christ freed us, he meant us to remain free" (Gal 5:1).
Sin is an act whereby a human person closes his/her spiritual
ears of conscience to God's Word. Such a person no longer

wishes to be present in surrendering love to God's loving presence according to the Word, Jesus Christ. Although we can never prevent God from being free to love us perfectly in self-giving through the Word made flesh, it is we who can run away from that presence and hide (Gn 3:10).

Sin brings about the loss of *eleutheria* by our seeking to rule our own life in complete independence. The ability to be free to choose life or death can never be lost in us, even when we choose to be enslaved to sin. What sin does is to harden our hearts. It keeps us away from God as the Center of our lives and all our choices. Through sin we begin our long pilgrimage in exile, absent to God who is ever present to us. God continually speaks his Word, but we remain deaf. The Trinity is present, touching us in millions of ways, yet we are blinded to God's presence.

Yet God is a consuming fire of love (Heb 12:29), ever reminding us of our primal dignity as persons created "according to God's image and likeness" (Gn 1:26).

God's Merciful Love

Various Hebrew words are used to describe God's pursuing love in terms of a condescending mercy that partakes of very rich and nuanced insights into God's freedom and forgiving love. *Aheb* is the Hebrew word that expresses God's unconditional love.[9] It expresses the concept that God, in spite of the infidelities of the Israelites, continues to be a living and loving God, a Father true to his everlasting covenant.

> If Yahweh set his heart on you and chose you, it was not because you outnumbered other peoples. You were the least of all peoples. It was for love of you…
> that Yahweh brought you out with his mighty hand

and redeemed you from the house of slavery, from the
power of Pharaoh, king of Egypt. Know then that
Yahweh, your God, is God indeed, the faithful God
who is true to his covenant and his graciousness for a
thousand generations.... (Dt 7:7-10)

This divine graciousness is underlined by the use of the
word *hen*. This stresses the unmerited quality of God's love for
human beings. He is under no obligation to bestow his kindness.
He remains always completely free in his mercy and loving care,
to give these or not to humankind. But it is the richly nuanced
word *hesed* that leads us into an idea of the freedom of God's love
for us. The emphasis in the word *hesed* is God's persistence and
devotion of love.[10]

Hesed is the act of loving kindness on God's part in
choosing Israel. Through his promises to use his might and
mercy to support his people a Covenant is made. This is
strikingly brought out in the tender words that Yahweh
addresses to his spouse, Israel:

I will betroth you to myself forever, betroth you with
integrity and justice, with tenderness and love; I will
betroth you to myself with faithfulness, and you will
come to know Yahweh. (Ho 2:19-20)

Jesus, the New Hesed Covenant

How beautiful and humbling is the realization among
Christians that the *Hesed* Covenant reaches its peak in
manifesting God's love for all of his children and his infinite,
merciful fidelity when his Word becomes incarnate. Jesus Christ
whose blood was poured out on the cross, not to pay back to the
heavenly Father an infinite debt we could never pay back, but to

show forth the perfect image of the invisible God (Col 1:15), is the New Covenant.

God so loved the world as to give us his only Son to be the way, the truth and the life leading us to salvation (Jn 3:16; 14:6):

> God's love for us was revealed
> when God sent into the world his only Son
> so that we could have life through him;
> this is the love I mean:
> not our love for God,
> but God's love for us when he sent his Son
> to be the sacrifice that takes our sins away. (1 Jn 4:9-10)

Jesus is God's eternal pledge of loving fidelity. In Jesus God could say that he "can have no greater love than to lay down his life for his friends. You are my friends" (Jn 15:13-14). Such *hesed* love of condescending mercy unto the last drop of blood is translated by St. Paul from the rich nuances of the Hebrew word into the Greek word *charis*.[11]

> But God loves us with so much love that he was
> generous with his mercy: when we were dead through
> our sins, he brought us to life with Christ — it is
> through grace (*charis* in Greek) that you have been
> saved — and raised us up with him and gave us a
> place with him in heaven, in Christ Jesus. (Eph 2:4-6)

The Mystery of God's Grace

Now we are able to understand through Scripture and the writings of the early Fathers of the Church that grace is not primarily a created *thing*. Grace is the loving, energetic relationship which results when the Father in his Son through his loving Spirit breaks into our human world in an *eternal now* act of love-unto-death. The remembrance of God's great protective, loving exploits that the prophets and the psalmists exhorted their people to recall in order to open themselves up to God's saving power is now in the New Testament the *anamnesis* of the Mass, the remembering of Jesus' gift of himself to us on the cross: "Do this as a memorial of me" (Lk 22:19).

Jesus, one with the Father and the Holy Spirit, is always freely emptying himself for each of us by dying on the cross in each salvific moment when we remember that he is the eternal image of the Father's perfect freedom and love in and through the Holy Spirit (Gal 2:20). In the new *Hesed* that is Jesus, love cannot remain uninvolved in the sufferings of his beloved people.

God's Loving Energies

Through the scriptural and patristic doctrine of the Trinity, as one in essence but now conceived of as "God for us," we can begin to appreciate the good news that God so loves us that, as Father, Son and Holy Spirit, he gives himself in everlasting actions called "divine energies of love." St. Basil writes that we know God only by means of his actions or energies:

> We say that we know our God by his energies. We do not affirm that we can approach the essence itself. His energies come down to us, but his essence remains unapproachable.[12]

The energies of God flow out from the three Persons, Father, Son and Holy Spirit. They are real (although not material nor merely an intellectual concept). They are *essential,* i.e. not an accident, but truly flow from the very essence of the mutually shared Godhead. Yet they are distinct from the actual being of the essence of God. These energies are essentially personified. They are the entire Trinity acting in loving relationships toward all creatures.

In such a vision, consistently taught by the Eastern Fathers, we readily understand that for them God can never be considered as static in his activities toward us and his created worlds. Because the energies are personalized, they are a common manifestation of the Persons of the Trinity. If God's energies were not personalized, we would not truly share in God's very own life through the Persons of Father, Son and Holy Spirit each in self-giving in one, unified essence. We would not be truly regenerated and made sharers of God's very own life (2 P 1:4). Grace, then, would be a "thing" that God heaps upon us when we do something to receive it. If God loves us and freely gives us a "thing" then we could never be in God's own image and likeness freely loving others as Jesus Christ and the Father love us.[13]

Our Greatest Dignity

Our greatest dignity consists in being called by the Trinity to share in the very nature of the triune God. We are capable of freely receiving God's communications and responding to the divine call to become *divinized* children of so loving a Father (1 Jn 3:1).

The redemptive work of the crucified and risen Jesus consists in giving us his Spirit of love through whom we may know the Father and the fullness of the Son (Jn 17:3). Thus we ourselves can become true children of God (Jn 1:12; Rm 8:15; Gal 4:6). This "going-forth" of God is simply grace in its

primal sense. We are eternally and infinitely loved by the
Father, Son and Holy Spirit. It is God in his *hesed,* covenantal
love, pursuing his people as the heavenly Father stretches out
his "two hands — Jesus Christ and the Holy Spirit" in the
words of St. Irenaeus of the second century.[14]

All of God's creative, loving energies are focused upon
the mystery of the Trinity's free choice of all of us to become
holy people in Christ Jesus (Eph 1:4-7). Now in the next
chapter we can prayerfully consider how God's love and
freedom have become manifest to us through the Word of God
made flesh for us, so that "...to all who did accept him, he gave
power to become children of God.... And we saw his glory, the
glory that is his as the only Son of the Father, full of grace and
truth" (Jn 1:12, 14).

Chapter Three

Jesus — The Freest of All Human Beings

Jesus is seen in the Synoptic Gospels as asking his disciples: "Who do you say I am?" (Mt 16:16). He continues to ask us in the silence of our hearts the same question. Do we have the correct image of Jesus as the perfect image of the unseen God (Col 1:15)? Down through the 2,000 years of Christianity we can discover an astonishing variety of images of Jesus.

The writer, Malachi Martin, presents us with a collection of Jesus figures that developed down through the ages.[1] Besides the non-Christian Jesus figures of Jesus-Jew from about 50 AD and Jesus-Muslim (from about the 7th century), in the early and middle ages Jesus was worshiped as Jesus-Caesar, Jesus-Monk, Jesus-Emperor, Jesus-Pantocrator, Jesus-Theologian and Jesus-Torquemada (of the 16th century Inquisition).

Following the Protestant Reformers, Jesus figures developed to meet the emotional needs of the 18th and 19th centuries. There is the Sweet Jesus, Jesus-Jehovah's Witness, Jesus-Christian Scientist, Jesus-Pentecostal, Jesus-Yogi. For the more "reasonable" Christians there evolved such Jesus images as Jesus-Apollo, Jesus-Goodfellow, Jesus the Revolutionary, Jesus-the Marxist, Jesus-Black, Jesus-Feminist, Jesus-Gay, Jesus-Superstar, Jesus the Buddhist, etc.

Jesus — The Freest Man

But the image of Jesus that rings truest to the Gospels and the Jesus encountered by his first followers and the one most modern persons desperately search for in their own personal lives is that of Jesus the Free Man. The most visible element of his personality, according to many, modern New Testament exegetes, is his freedom.[2] Christian Duquoc agrees with such scripture scholars when he writes: "Jesus behaves as a free man, free before God and for God; free before man and for man."[3]

The freedom of Jesus cannot be understood except in his relationship to his heavenly Father. This is why we began this book by stressing in Chapter One the inter-trinitarian community of love of the Father, Son and Holy Spirit before this love became incarnated in Jesus Christ, the God-Man. Let us now examine how Jesus grew in freedom as he grew in wisdom and knowledge and grace before God and man (Lk 2:52).

Jesus Grew Daily in Greater Freedom
Before His Heavenly Father

Before Jesus could preach freedom and bring liberation to his listeners, he had to grow daily in his personal life experiences to encounter the heavenly Father's freeing love in all his human situations. Anyone, who can call others to be their true selves, must first be in complete control of himself. Jesus gives credit for his authority and freedom to the Holy Spirit and his heavenly Father. We cannot understand how Jesus effects his goal to "set captives free" until we study how he is "the freest of human beings."

Luke the Evangelist has Jesus beginning his mission of bringing freedom to the captives with his reading of the prophecy of Isaiah in the synagogue in Nazareth:

The spirit of the Lord has been given to me,
for he has anointed me.

He has sent me to bring the good news to the poor,
to proclaim liberty to captives
and to the blind new sight,
to set the downtrodden free,
to proclaim the Lord's year of favor.

(Lk 4:18-19; Is 61:1-2)

The Freedom of Jesus

The freedom of Jesus cannot be understood except in his relationship to his heavenly Father. Jesus grew ever freer as he turned inwardly and there found at the center of his being the ever-loving Father: "I am in the Father and the Father is in me" (Jn 14:11). Joy, ecstasy, peace and bliss poured over Jesus as he became more aware of the Father's free gift of himself to his beloved Son. Through the ever-binding love of the Holy Spirit Jesus returns the free gift of himself to the Father.

It was in the long hours of deep, contemplative prayer during his thirty years at Nazareth and his prayer on the mountain tops and in the deserts during his public years where Jesus, alone with the Father, learned how to become more and more his own person, progressively more and more free. It was in their union as they embraced, surrounded each other like a mother covering her baby, like two lovers made one in ecstatic embrace, that Jesus experienced the fullness of human freedom.

Wrapped in the Father's consuming fire of love, Jesus could only whisper as he would during his public life and finally on the cross: "Take all, Father, as you wish. I seek only to please you in all things." In that *eternal now* gaze of the

Father, Jesus rose to ever new levels of awareness that he was
sheer gift from the Father.

No separation could keep Jesus from the Father. He was
always "at home" with the Father, "nearest the heart of the
Father" (Jn 1:18). Jesus reveals on each page of the four
Gospels his freedom from any doubt about his own inner
identity and therefore his assurance in regard to the goal of his
earthly life. He knows clearly his origin and his mission on
earth.

> I have come from heaven...
> to do the will of the One who sent me. (Jn 7:16)

I Must Be About My Father's Business

A thing most difficult for many Christians is to
understand that Jesus was totally human. He was the pre-
existent Word of God who became flesh. Yet he lived most of
his life in obscurity in Nazareth as the son of a humble
carpenter, Joseph. He was as human as you and I are and,
therefore, subject to all human laws of growth. When Mary
and Joseph, after searching in Jerusalem for the lost Jesus,
found him in the Temple and asked him why did he do this to
them, he simply replied, "Did you not know that I must be
busy with my Father's affairs?" (Lk 2:49-50).

Tradition tells us that Jesus spent most of his earthly life
hidden in an insignificant corner of Galilee, in Nazareth.
Thirty out of his thirty-three years spent in such a hidden life
could seem to have been a waste of his powers to preach to the
multitudes, to announce the inbreaking of God's Kingdom on
earth and to heal the broken in body, soul and spirit. What
took place in Nazareth was Jesus' growing into a fully realized
personality who would humble himself by becoming totally

submissive to the will of his Divine Father whom he progressively experienced in his humanity as dwelling intimately within himself.

He had a human body as we have, with its physical and psychic faculties. He hungered and thirsted, required sleep, had sexual powers which he needed to discipline along with intellectual, emotional and volitional endowments. "We have one who has been tempted in every way that we are, though he is without sin" (Heb 4:15). He had to discover in every facet of his humanity the presence of God and to yield that part of his being in loving obedience to his Father. He had to learn to allow God to be God as he tempered his human will to the divine power that was at his command.

It would be his human hands that would touch a leper and heal him, and that experience of using his hands in loving touch was an experience he had to learn. His human voice learned to speak to the heavenly Father as he would one day on the cross, crying out in total surrender and abandonment to his loving Father. His human intelligence pondered over the scriptures of his ancestors. In his village synagogue his mind would be the instrument for communicating God's divine message to human beings. He had to study that message and experience it in the marrow of his bones.

It was at Nazareth in those hidden years that Jesus learned how to move freely according to the inspirations of the Holy Spirit dwelling within him. This meant for Jesus disciplining his will to please God the Father in every thought, word and deed. He learned to surrender to the powerful current of God's love flowing strongly and gently throughout all his life. In a word, he was progressing daily in freedom by uniting his will to the Father's in total surrender of himself to please the Father.

Living a Poor and Simple Life

Jesus grew in freedom as he learned to rejoice and to give thanks to the Father, the Giver of all things. His simple needs he discovered as gifts provided by his loving Father. His poverty was not only physical but also psychological and spiritual. Jesus lived his earthly life in the conviction that he was most radically and ontologically a *non-being* in his humanity except for God's outpoured love in unselfish creation.

Over and over Jesus confessed that of himself he was nothing:

> The Son can do nothing by himself;
> he can do only what he sees the Father doing:
> and whatever the Father does, the Son does too.
> (Jn 5:19)[4]

Jesus' magnificent obsession throughout his entire earthly life was centered around doing only his Father's will. As he taught us in the Lord's Prayer, so he lived: "Your will be done, on earth as in heaven" (Mt 6:10). His freedom to do always the will of the Father will be seen in his public life. Let us see how Jesus had the courage and the authority to express his perfect freedom in all of his relationships toward others. But this is possible only because Jesus exercised this freedom in the exercise of the Spirit's infused faith, hope and love.

Living in Faith

We cannot come into God's real world without his Spirit's infusion of the gift of faith. The same applied to Jesus as he sought always in freedom to take charge of his life and give it back to the heavenly Father in total self-giving. He built his relationships with God and neighbor on loving service, confident of the Father's perfect and free love toward him. His human faith grew in his prayerful encounters with the Father's freeing love that gave him the power to return his love in service toward others.

Faith removed for Jesus the veils found in most other creatures that hide the face of God behind so many false distortions. It revealed to Jesus the redemptive plan of God in every occurrence and in every human action. Faith revealed to Jesus the Father in all creatures and all creatures in God.

Faith Calls for a Loving Response

Jesus developed confidence in his responses to do the will of God as perfectly and as freely as he could humanly do it. The most basic faith-response in loving surrender to God was, for Jesus, to lovingly obey the will of the Father in the clear expressions of the ten commandments handed down through Moses and whatever else Jesus understood to be a command of the Father. We can see this in his agony in the Garden of Gethsemane and as he hung dying slowly on the cross of Calvary.

In the life of Jesus there were areas of free choices made by him in response to the loving presence of his Father. These decisions were made sometimes very spontaneously, sometimes with reflection, sometimes in deep, silent prayer. Not only did Jesus seek to do whatever his Father commanded, but, in his freedom, he also sought to return his love by being sensitive to seek in all things to do the slightest wish of the Father. For this he moved under the power of the Spirit in ever greater submission and surrender.

Yet Jesus shows us an even higher degree of love in freedom by going beyond trying to satisfy his heavenly Father's wishes to seeking in all things ways to please him.

Even in human love we can bring ourselves from time to time
to forget ourselves, and in a burst of self-sacrifice for the one we
love, we can "improvise" some gift that costs us a price to
"enflesh" our love. We can freely choose to make this sacrifice,
under no obligation through an expressed command or even a
wish on the part of the one we love. Jesus, who had experienced
in his humanity the freely given love of the Father, would to
that degree wish to do something special in return, in freely
given love, to please the Father: "He who sent me is with me,
and has not left me to myself, but I always do what pleases
him" (Jn 8:29). This can be called "creative suffering," the
essence of true love, as we will see in his freely chosen death on
the cross.

Freed from Pharisaism

Rooted in the truth, Jesus was free from any
heteronomous spirit that would have tied him slavishly to the
existing religious doctrines and practices that had become a
binding force among the Jews of his time. His Father wanted
all human beings to be freed and Jesus fought against any
religious, idolatrous forms and institutions that would prevent
human beings from worshiping God alone.[5]

Jesus discovered the Father working at all times (Jn 5:17)
and this colored his own approach toward Jewish law and
ordinances and his teaching to others about how they should
regard such extrinsic norms. He was faithful in attending
services in synagogues and in the Temple in Jerusalem. He
healed the lepers and charged them to fulfill the ceremonies
required by law (Lk 5:14; 17:14). He paid the Temple tax (Mt
17:27). He came not to destroy the law (Mt 5:17), but to fulfill
it (Mt 3:15).

But in other matters concerning religious practices

enjoined by the religious leaders of his time, Jesus could be
quite indifferent and even commit violations. He freed himself
and others from the abuses concerning the Sabbath rest that a
casuistry inflicted as an unreasonable burden on the people. He
healed on the Sabbath and thus showed the Pharisees that the
Sabbath was for the works of God. God would not allow a day
to pass if healing were imminently possible to the sick in Jesus'
very presence, and thus he willed to bring the Father's healing
to those in need.

Jesus knew himself to be the end and the goal of the law.
He was even what the Temple was all about and, once his body
was destroyed (Jn 2:19), there would be no need for the material
Temple made of stones at Jerusalem. All blood sacrifices were
to prepare for his supreme sacrifice of blood unto the remission
of sins (Mt 26:28).

Purification of the outside of the vessel had no meaning if
one's heart was not cleansed by compunction and conversion
(Mk 7:15). Evil was not in any of God's creatures, but only in
the heart of the individual human person.

Jesus Is the New Law

Jesus touched people, looked upon them, loved them,
spoke to them. His humanity was the point of encounter with
God, as once in the desert the tabernacle was the point from
whence the life of God could flow into the lives of all who
accepted him. Jesus manifested his freedom in the authority by
which he preached those sublime teachings that were the
brightness of God's own truth, truths that would turn his
listeners from the darkness of the ungodly and the sinful into
children born, not of flesh, but "of God himself" (Jn 1:13).

Jesus was aware that he was now the New Law, replacing
the Torah. For as the Israelites received God's life and truth

through the Jewish Law given them by Moses, now life and
truth have become incarnate in the person of Jesus Christ:

> Indeed, from his fullness we have, all of us received —
> yes, grace in return for grace,
> since, though the Law was given through Moses,
> grace and truth have come through Jesus Christ.
> No one has ever seen God;
> it is the only Son,
> who is nearest to the Father's heart,
> who has made him known. (Jn 1:16-18)

Free To Be Human

Jesus could afford to be freely human since all human
beings, in God's eternal design, are created according to his
image and likeness. No human consciousness ever grew
progressively by "revealing" the Father's immense, personal
love for human beings as did that of Jesus. "As the Father has
loved me, so I have loved you" (Jn 15:9). Jesus insisted before
his disciples: "To have seen me is to have seen the Father" (Jn
14:9).

F. Malmberg writes about the God-Man:

> In other words, it implies that real humanity exists in
> him in a supernatural, super-human, divine-human
> way, that Christ is "Man" in the way that only God
> can be: in Mersch's phrase, "divinely human."[6]

Openness to All Others

Freed from all insecurity before his heavenly Father and all
other human beings whom he encountered, Jesus spontaneously

opened himself completely to each person, whether friend or enemy, and loved them with the same love that his Father had for them. All aggressive, nervous moods were dispelled by the gentle love with which Jesus loved each person. His eyes were mirrors that reflected the loving gaze of the Eternal Father. His touch upon the maimed, the demon-possessed, the sinner or a beloved friend brought the healing power of God into all who accepted his love.

Thus at each moment Jesus was freed from anxieties and worries as he opened himself to cooperate with the loving activity of his Father. He was freed from all impatience at his own human limitations, at the failures and sinfulness of those around him, including his disciples. He possessed a marvelous freedom of heart, a spontaneity and completely at-homeness with the given human scene.

Yet his openness to be guided by the Spirit of his Father gave him also an inner self-discipline, even an austerity, in his relationships with all human beings, especially his beloved friends. His mother, disciples and friends were not his ultimate concern:

> He did not merely use them as instruments to glorify
> the Father, but they were diaphanous points of
> finding the Father in the human context and to
> return love to him by serving each human person
> encountered.[7]

There was that inner sanctuary in his *heart*, where he was most himself; freed of any selfishness, wanting to have only his Father as the perfect center of his life, of all affections and desires. At the converging of his will with that of his Father, Jesus was able to swing freely from all that is temporal, finite, of this created world, and drown himself in the *eternal now* of the Father's being. There Jesus grew into freedom. There the Father shared with him his very own freedom, to love the world and each human being as a point of self-surrender in perfect love.

Freedom To Become Holy

To describe God's holiness is to touch the "insideness" of God. But in its essence as freedom and love, the Trinity manifests itself as good, beautiful and self-giving. It is God in the totality of his being, moving outwardly toward the other, toward created human beings and angels, to offer himself as a gift, sharing his own divine nature with us. Jesus came to reveal God's holiness. What is God's holiness like? It is like the holiness of Jesus, the God-Man.

His holiness consisted first in his having been sanctified by the Holy Spirit. Jesus was the gift of the Father through the Spirit. He can do nothing of himself, but only from what he receives from his Father through the Spirit of freedom and love (2 Cor 3:17). Jesus was no automaton without free will to cooperate with the will of the Father. He had to will to be holy as the Father is holy.

The first manifestation of his holiness consists in Jesus' freedom from any sin. His disciples and even his enemies witnessed to this, but he himself forcefully speaks of himself as sinless. John the Baptist received a vision of the Lamb of God as spotless, who was to take away the sins of the world (Jn 1:29-30). Jesus claimed there is no injustice, no iniquity in himself (Jn 7:18). He always did what pleased the Father (Jn 8:29). Satan had no power over him (Jn 14:30).

Jesus threw out to the Pharisees the daring challenge: "Can any of you convict me of sin?" (Jn 8:46). Only holiness, true freedom from sin at all times and in all circumstances, could claim this. Because he was sinless, he could forgive sins as God could. He could also delegate this power to his disciples since his Father had given him the power of judgment and his judgment is true (Mt 9:2; Mk 2:3; Lk 5:18; 17:47; 23:43; Jn 5:14; 8:11). His blood would be "poured out for the remission of sins" (Lk 22:20; Mt 26:28; Mk 14:24).

Jesus, Tempted as We

The holiness of Jesus is seen, not only as the presence of the Father's Spirit in him, giving him strength to unmask and defeat the Devil, but also as a growing process which brings holiness to him as he confronts the Evil One and conquers him. At the core of his temptations was the struggle, as we also must battle against the same, between a state of pride and independence or to live in free surrender and loving obedience to the Father's will. Freedom is won by this battle wherein our isolated self surrenders to our true self in love, freely given to God who freely loves us eternally. This freedom came fully to Jesus only in the *exodus* experience on the cross as Jesus passed over from gift received to gift returned to the Father.

Jesus Freely Serves All of Us Human Beings

Jesus, poor, humble and loving, shows forth his holiness as he images in human form the invisible Father by his active service toward all human beings. He came to serve because that is free love in action and he was acting out in a human way the Father's love for all his children made in the image and likeness of Christ. He, who was one with God in glory, did not cling to that dignity, but rather he emptied himself, taking on himself our humanity (Ph 2:6 ff). He who was the master washed the feet of his disciples (Jn 13:1-16).

He lived a life of total self-denial and obedience to his Father. Thus he went forth with complete availability, giving himself to each person as he saw his Father doing. The Father's compassion for his children drove Jesus to act out that compassion. He never sought his own comfort when others needed him. He burned with an inner fire to actualize the presence of the Father in freedom and perfect love in the lives of all the human beings Jesus met. "I have come to bring fire to the earth, and how I wish it were blazing already!" (Lk 12:49).

Jesus serves most by not only preaching about the Father's love, but also by freely acting out this love. Throughout all his public life, Jesus went about doing good, especially in the form of healing all types of sickness and diseases. He is never more the perfect image of the heavenly Father than when he saw the multitude fainting and being scattered abroad as sheep without a shepherd. And he was moved with mercy and compassion (Mt 9:36).

Jesus Acquires Freedom in His Prayer

The Evangelists have grasped the intrinsic relation of Jesus' prayer and his freedom. From their descriptions of Jesus in prayerful communion with his Father we note that Jesus never prays as a means to run away from his life-situation or to seek merely the consolations of the Father. Nor is he totally absorbed in praying for whatever would make him a more powerful *doer* of God's will.

The prayer of Jesus is tied intrinsically with the coming of God's Kingdom. Luke presents Jesus as praying to his Father in what regards his mission, the fulfillment of his Father's salvific plan for all of his creation. Jesus prays at his baptism (Lk 3:21), in the desert (Lk 5:16), before Peter's confession that he is the Son of the living God (Lk 9:18), in a moment of joy filled by the

Holy Spirit (Lk 10:21), before teaching his disciples the Lord's Prayer (Lk 11:1), that Peter be strengthened (Lk 22:31), in the Garden of Gethsemane (Lk 22:39-46) and he prays on the cross (Lk 23:34, 46).

He seeks the face of his Father in praise and thanksgiving, in petitions that follow from his free desire to help bring about God's Kingdom. In prayer Jesus touches the freedom and holiness of the Father and is filled with a like freedom and love to serve the Father.

Jesus Is Love

Jesus becomes progressively more holy as his heavenly Father is holy because, in a word, he is filled with the Father's love, the Holy Spirit. Other characteristics of his holiness are summarized in the one phrase: Jesus is love. The free love of God conquers in him at the peak of his filial obedience and complete abandonment of himself to the Father in freely dying on our behalf. He grows progressively more free and more loving as he seeks always to give up his own will in order lovingly to do his Father's will. He acquired more and more freedom and love as he sought to obey the Father, even unto death (Ph 2:8).

> Although he was Son, he learned to obey through
> suffering; but, having been made perfect, he became
> for all who obey him the source of eternal salvation
> and was acclaimed by God with the title of high priest
> of the order of Melchizedek. (Heb 5:8-10)

Love unto Death

The depths of Jesus' free suffering, especially on the cross, can be understood only in terms of the infinite and free love he received in his human consciousness from his heavenly Father. Love begets love, and suffering begets suffering. On the cross on which he freely emptied himself totally out of love for the Father on our behalf, Jesus chose the most perfect sign of the infinite love of God for each of us. Jesus on the cross was choosing to be in the human form of suffering, freely accepted out of love of the Father and of us, what God is always like in his love for us.

When Jesus cried out in the agonizing pain and darkest abandonment of the cross, "My God, my God, why have you deserted me?" (Mk 15:34), God's love and freedom was perfectly expressed in the human term of suffering unto death. Jesus had said: "The Father loves me because I lay down my life in order to take it up again. No one takes it from me. I lay it down of my own free will" (Jn 10:17-18). The Father loves Jesus because he, the Word of God incarnate, lays down his life freely in order to express definitively God's eternal love for humankind. With such perfect love which Jesus expressed so powerfully in dying for us, he shows us how ardently he wishes us to be set free.

Chapter Four

Broken and Enslaved

God Trinity whispered in the silence of a muted, material
world of beauty and multiplicity that he wanted to be
recognized and accepted by other creatures with whom he
could share his very own life.

> Let us make man in our own image, in the likeness
> of ourselves... in the image of God he created him,
> male and female he created them. (Gn 1:26-27)

God dug deeply into the very core of his being, the triune
community of Father, Son and Holy Spirit, and put into the
hearts of the first man and woman and in all their progeny, you
and me, their very own burning love for each other. But
because we are created by God as finite, material human
beings, God puts into us also a burning yearning, a deep down,
aching pain, to know the triune family of God and to share
intimately in their Spirit of love in a unity-of-difference.

This is what St. Augustine was referring to when he wrote
in his *Confessions:* "...for Thou hast formed us for Thyself,
and our hearts are restless till they find rest in Thee."[1] We
roam throughout this material world of ours, searching to
discover more intimately the *I-Thou-We* of God's Community
in every flower we touch. In every sunset we cry out to God

with awe and reverence: "Oh, God!" Nothing, not even the
oneness we experience in our human loves through the
uniqueness of our *two-ness* and our *otherness,* can ever take away
this longing, aching pain within the depths of our being. We
hunger for greater oneness in the triuneness of God and for our
uniqueness as a beautiful manifestation of God's presence on
this earth in the incarnation of our "fleshness" with God's
presence.

Law of Inner Growth

As we have already seen in previous chapters, by being
made according to God's image and likeness, we possess the
ability to stretch ourselves upward to attain new levels of
transcendent meaningfulness by letting go of lower levels of
being. Holy Scripture presents this conversion process in terms
of an *exodus,* a passing-over to a state of becoming progressively
free in the darkness and sterility of the desert that leads us to the
promised land.

Psychologists speak of it as a twofold movement. The first
stage consists in accepting ourselves with honesty and without
excuse. This is an awakening moment, revealing the truth that
what we thought was our true personhood was in reality a false
self. Many of us seek various ways of escaping this self-
knowledge, such as excessive busyness with our work or travel
or merely in becoming couch potatoes!

Only if we learn to accept sincerely our existential self can
we ever hope to open up to the second movement, namely, to
hunger and thirst in the totality of our being to share in God's
divine life. We desire passionately to be someone more noble,
more loving, more one with God and neighbor and the entire
universe. This is the *élan* toward new life and greater freedom.
This True Being calls us to experience our true selves in the

Source of all being, as a unique manifestation of God's presence in human form on this earth.

But this can only follow the letting go of the false self and all the protective devices and techniques we have been using to secure the lie that the illusory person is our true self. And how most of us human beings detest the thought of the dying process that will yield to new life! How we are afraid to enter into the depths of our unconscious in order that we might become more conscious of our beautiful, unique self as we bring the brokenness in our heart to the healing power of Love itself.

Breaking the False Idols

In the words of Gabriel Marcel, the French philosopher and dramatist, such a person "has become once and for all a question for himself."[2] The most important question we must ask ourselves daily is: "Will we stay inside ourselves, groping for ways in which we can let God set us free from our imprisonment and heal us of our brokenness instead of running 'outside' to be diverted from the call to new life of greater love and freedom?" Marcel describes our habitual response to God's call to break the false idols within us:

> When we are at rest, we find ourselves almost inevitably put in the presence of our own inner emptiness, and this very emptiness is in reality intolerable to us. But there is more; there is the fact that through this emptiness we inevitably become aware of the misery of our condition, a "condition so miserable," says Pascal, "that nothing can console us when we think about it carefully." Hence the necessity of diversion.[3]

Inner Brokenness

Sin in Holy Scripture and in the writings of the Eastern Christian Fathers is any brokenness, regardless of the cause that impedes the life of the indwelling Trinity from having its full sway in our life. This brokenness touches us as an individual. It has old and far-reaching causes stemming, not only directly from our parents, but through their lineage back through preceding generations of our ancestors, even back to Adam and Eve.

Effects are registered within our being, our mode of thinking, and ways of acting that come from the world in which we live and from the historical roots of that world extending back to the beginning of human history. Truly we can say with the repentant King David: "You know I was born guilty, a sinner from the moment of my conception" (Ps 51:5).

To accept our history and all that has constituted any obstacles to receiving the full life that Jesus has come to bring us (Jn 10:10) is healthy and leads to our happiness. For our history is the existential place and point in time where God wishes to meet us. Now is the time of salvation through inner healing that will lead us to greater freedom and love of God and neighbor. Such self-knowledge of our brokenness is the necessary first step toward that healing and liberation from our enslavement to the dark and hidden forces within each of us. This is what Jesus called his listeners to embrace: a *metanoia*, a conversion that stems from an honest disgust with eating the "husks of swine" (Lk 15:16) and a humble desire to cry out to God for inner healing. In prayer God's Spirit will reveal to us, in the abyss of our darkness and sin, what we are existentially as we stand before him in our inner poverty.

Unless we can open up these lower layers of our psyche to God's inner healing, we will always remain wounded and crippled psychically and spiritually; a helpless victim of primordial forces within and around us. We may desire to become a holier person, full of love and freedom to live only to glorify God Trinity. Yet, the first step in that direction is to confront the glitzy idols, the golden calves we have fashioned in the furnace of fire out of the trinkets and baubles of fool's gold and silver, as the Israelites did in the Sinai Desert (Ex 33:1-5).

In this chapter let us sincerely and humbly seek through the overshadowing of the Holy Spirit to examine our brokenness, our sinfulness, our lack of genuine faith, hope and love that have held us in bondage. In Chapter Five, then, we will bring our broken selves to Jesus Christ, the risen Lord, who alone through his Triune love and freedom can heal us and set us free.

There Is Sin in Our Members

There is not one who reads these words who cannot claim his or her share of brokenness and enslavement to the "unspiritual self" in us as St. Paul wrote to the Romans: "…but I am unspiritual; I have been sold as a slave to sin" (Rm 7:14). The ancient Greeks referred to the *daemon* or *daimon* within all of us. This refers both to the light and the darkness inside of us. We have both positive and negative elements stored up in giant proportions to be actualized in creative or destructive words and deeds. We all veer dizzily, now toward madness, then at times toward noble love and again toward cruel selfishness.

The demonic in all of us can be good or evil. Often it is a bit of both. It is never totally oriented toward beauty and creativity. We are never in this life totally free to do always, not our will, but that of God. Dr. Rollo May, the popular American author and psychoanalyst, gives us a keen insight in his explanation of the demonic in us:

There lie in these words *(devil* from the Greek verb,
diabollein and *symbol* from the Greek verb, *sym-
bolein)* tremendous implications with respect to an
ontology of good and evil. The *symbolic* is that which
draws together, ties, integrates the individual in
himself and with his group; the *diabolic,* in contrast,
is that which disintegrates and tears apart. Both of
these are present in the demonic.[4]

We Are a Part of a Broken World

From Scripture and human history we learn that we form
a solidarity with the whole world in our brokenness and
enslavement, in "the sin of the world." We find our darkness to
be a part of the world's darkness that "from the beginning until
now the entire creation, as we know, has been groaning in one
great act of giving birth…" (Rm 8:22-23). You and I are
individuals who have become what we are and what we will be
through our actions upon and reactions to other individual
persons. Our parents, friends, teachers, wife, husband,
children, enemies and even indifferent acquaintances have
contributed to make us what we are by their attitudes, acts and
even omissions. It is here that we come face to face with the
daemonic in all of us, that which is part of our broken state of
inauthenticity and also that which explains the good and the
creative in our lives with its great potential for even such
greater beauty in the future.

Like Tennyson's *Ulysses,* in all of our travels from the
first moment of conception until this present moment and even
to the end of our earthly existence, we can say: "I am a part of
all that I have met."

Interrelationships

The interdependence on others, not only for our being, but for our being such and such a person, is testified today by microbiology. We inherit in birth, not only the values of our parents, but through them the values of generations and generations that preceded them. What an amazing world of interrelationships science opens up to us! Each of the 100 trillion cells in our body contains about 100,000 different genes, composed of DNA (deoxyribonucleic acid). Each DNA molecule stores coded information to be used to sustain and duplicate itself. Through such dependency upon our parents, we receive more than similar physical traits. We are also recipients of much of their positive and negative qualities. We share in their brokenness even before we see the light of day.

Not Free To Love

We crave above all else in life to love and to be loved. But pitifully the mounting rate of lonely persons committing physical or psychological suicides, the increase of broken marriages that end in divorce after divorce, the inability of so many parents to relate lovingly to their children and the children to their parents, all point out how unfree we human beings are to love and receive love.

What inner brokenness we experience in what God meant to be both the most human and divine experience for us, namely, human love! We sincerely tell our loved ones that we really want to love them. But as we enter into the depths of ourselves and others, opening ourselves to them, we experience fear and doubt. We dread a true confrontation with our unredeemed, hidden areas as we see ourselves being mirrored in the openness of the other.

Demands of sensitivity and fidelity not known before are made as we receive the gift of the other. Self can no longer be the center, but we must seek humbly to serve only the unique godliness in the other. True love makes terrifying demands on us to let the other be completely her/himself. My selfish needs must yield to the godly desire to seek only to serve the uniqueness in the other, that which will fulfill the other's true self.

The Agony of Losing Our Control

What agony to let go and not hold on to the other! What fear as my unreal self battles the hidden, potential true self, and I struggle between "using" others or "dying" to what is false in me to serve others in authentically free love. I can so easily insist that the other person measure up to my expectations, all too often to satisfy my selfish needs. In my selfishness I can lose the "symbolic," that which integrates and binds into a oneness, and I yield to the "diabolic," that which disintegrates and scatters.

I can lose the sense of wonder and mystery, poetry and transcendence by insisting that the other person be more the father or mother that I once needed to touch me and cuddle me.

The Unreal Self

As a result of the basic needs for caring persons to love us, especially when these needs were not fulfilled in early childhood, all of us have suffered what Dr. Arthur Janov terms "the primal pains."[5] We ache in the depths of our conscious and unconscious selves to have such basic needs satisfied. But worse, such pains create tensions and a split, according to Dr. Janov, between our *real* self, the subject of such desired needs, and our *unreal* self, that is created in defense to avoid greater pain.[6]

The unreal, enslaved self begins to emerge as the one that receives less of hurts. But this self begins to grow farther away from the real self that becomes more and more suppressed into the unconscious. We struggle then to live according to our unreal self because such an approach to life is initially less painful. We forget what it feels like to be spontaneous and free, because we have lived so long with our false self. In our pained insecurity we fight to maintain that image of ourselves as who we truly are.

This explains how very fiercely aggressive we can be when our unreal self is temporarily unmasked by others. We treat them who often really love us as though they were our great enemies. This is seen often in the hate-love ambivalence found often among married couples. How uncomfortable and defenseless we feel in the impotence of serious sickness, above all, before death, or even in times of a spiritual retreat away from our habitual environment. Hence we begin to role-play when our real self begins to show its head with a promise of what could be. Still we return sooner or later to "normalcy" and feel much better that things are as they always were.

Fears Rob Us of True Freedom

The opposite of love, deeply received, will always be tensioned fears that build up in our lives as a result of not being able to grow into our true self spontaneously in the ambience of love freely given. When we lack the healing experience of true love from God and neighbor, fears of all sorts take over to destroy any true integration. "In love there can be no fear, but fear is driven out by perfect love" (1 Jn 4:18).

Without love fears build up and become centered in the apprehension of a future danger. Unhappiness, doubt, anxiety, worry, dread, hatred, anger, horror, fright or terror at the thought of some impending evil weighs heavily upon our psyche and our body, crippling our growth and breaking down our health.

Fear can have countless objects. It is the state of fear from which we must be delivered. From such brokenness, regardless how such came about in our lives, we must be healed and made whole. And yet how deeply embedded into the fibers of our mind are the multitude of fears that hold us in slavery and lack of freedom.[7]

Unending Fears

The list of crippling fears is unending. There is the fear from human respect, an inferiority complex before more intelligent persons, those wealthier, more beautiful, more successful than we are. There is disgust regarding our own failures and fear of future failures. We may not be free because our character is too lopsidedly shy or too independently over-bearing. Our past habits, sins, thought patterns, our training and education, our parents and family life, the list in this direction is so unending of unfreeing factors that we humbly thank God that we are as normal as we seemingly appear to be!

How bound we are with unforgiveness and prejudices toward others![8] Who can describe the fears of the coming day's events that knot my spirit into a cord with which I beat myself mercilessly as a tyrant beats a slave into quivering submission? How I fear that sickness or some calamity may strike me today. I may be mugged. Cold fear of each unknown person I meet possesses me. I fear car, train or airplane accidents. Fear, fear, fear! God, come to my rescue!

Slavery to Addictions

Modern psychologists and psychiatrists help us to explore our brokenness and enslavement to our false selves by exploring the areas of our lives that are enslaved to what they term *addictions*.

Dr. Gerald G. May, MD, in his excellent book, *Addiction and Grace,* defines addictions that are so powerful in depriving us of our freedom to deliberately choose life in accord with God's salvific will:

> Addiction exists wherever persons are internally compelled to give energy to things that are not their true desires. To define it directly, addiction is a *state* of compulsion, obsession, or preoccupation that enslaves a person's will and desire. Addiction sidetracks and eclipses the energy of our desire for love and goodness. We succumb because our desire becomes attached, nailed, to specific behaviors, objects, or people. *Attachment,* then, is the process that enslaves desire and creates the state of addiction.[9]

Non-Attachment Leads to Freedom

To become "unattached" from our enslaving addictions, we must become "detached," the traditional, but very much misunderstood term used in the history of Christian asceticism. The Fathers and Mothers of the Eastern Christian desert spirituality called it *apatheia.*[10] The goal of *apatheia* is never to kill all desires and passions.[11] It strives to attain the state of true Christian freedom through virtue and the control of our inordinate passions, so that one might always act in harmonious obedience to do only God's will in all things.[12]

Hope in the Divine Physician

No one living on earth is without some brokenness and addiction. As we sense our own powerlessness to stretch out toward wholeness, we search desperately for some way to be delivered from the many forces within us and around us that hold us in constant enslavement. Is there someone who can say to us, as a certain healer long ago said to a paralytic, "Get up, and pick up your bed and go off home" (Mt 9:6)?

Out of the depths of our fears, guilt, doubts, frustrations, anger, loneliness and depression, we must learn to cry out to the Lord with the Psalmist:

> From the depths I call to you, Yahweh,
> Lord, listen to my cry for help.
> Listen compassionately
>   to my pleading! (Ps 130:1)

Freedom is the result of a process of growth as we learn to love all things in God and God in all things.[13] We can be set free by true faith and hope in God's active, guiding providence in our lives, even in the midst of our fears, brokenness, addictions and sins. Jesus is the Way that leads us to the Truth that our heavenly Father truly loves us as imaged by the love Jesus has shown for us. It is acting on this truth of God's infinite, perfect, active love for us in every moment of our human existence that will bring us peace, true healing and integration (Jn 14:6).

Since he is all-powerful, the Father can always take the initiative and act independently of us. Yet he respects our free will and seeks to "allure" us by his goodness to make decisions out of our inner dignity as his children. His providence continually watches over us and exercises a beneficent influence upon us through his grace at all times.

True children of God realize in life's circumstances that they have no strength of their own. Because we have been so filled with our long-embedded addictions and sinful self-centeredness, we are to confess our weakness to do good by ourselves. We know with St. Paul that all our strength is in God through Jesus Christ. True strength begins with the conviction that we are weak, but our very weakness confessed becomes our strength because we lovingly surrender to do God's will in all things (2 Cor 12:9).

We will find that our very enslavements and lack of freedom can be the human situations in which we can long to come home to God by positively asserting our total weakness and yet our total confidence and hope in God's grace. "It is, after all, the pure, naked aspiration of the human soul toward freedom and through freedom, to love."[14]

When Jesus confronted the broken ones, the maimed, the blind, lepers, paralytics, epileptics, the possessed, sinners living in the darkness of selfishness, bound by pride, hatred and self-indulgence, his love and compassionate mercy went out to them. He was the imaged love of the Father suffering to see his children suffer. So he healed all of them, provided they believed in him and accepted him as the Lord of their lives.

Let us now prayerfully see how Christ can free us from our slavery to live freely in loving others as we love ourselves in him.

Chapter Five

Jesus Sets Us Captives Free

We have already seen how Jesus Christ from all eternity preexisted in the ecstatic union of freedom and love with the Father and the Holy Spirit. We also pondered the great mystery of God's love, that "when we were dead through our sins, he brought us to life with Christ" (Eph 2:5). Jesus through his Holy Spirit during his earthly exodus grew daily in love and freedom in his seeking to do the Father's will. He lovingly accepted the plan of the Father by freely dying on the cross so that by his resurrectional presence he may give us a share in his divine-human love and perfect freedom through the gift of the Holy Spirit.

Now let us focus on how Jesus liberates us captives from our imprisonment. God pursues us in love. He gives us also the frightening power to say *yes* or *no* to this gift of freedom. We stand dizzily on the heights of the universe, tempted as Jesus was in the desert, to bow in loving surrender to God's majesty and tender love as our eternal Father or to walk away into the darkness of self-centered love.

Plato in the 4th century BC describes very well the human condition in *The Allegory of the Cave* from his classic, *The Republic.* He depicts human beings as being tied to each other, forced to sit in a dark cave below the earth, gazing on the wall in front of them at the dancing shadows beamed on it from

above. One day an enlightened person came into the cave from
above and told them that he was able to untie their bonds and set
them free. If they wished to follow him out of the cave, they
would discover a most beautiful world. They would feel the
warmth of the sun and instead of shadows and darkness they
would see radiant light bathing the multicolored flowers, trees,
singing birds and animals of all kinds in the world above. In
their fear of letting go of their darkness and illusory shadows
they refused to believe the enlightened guide from above and
instead chose to remain enslaved to the dark.

Jesus Comes to Our Aid

In a way Jesus is continually appearing as Light shining in
our darkness. This is the work of the risen Christ: to fulfill the
prophecies of old that God would heal his people of their
blindness. This invitation from the Trinity requires our full
cooperation. Bob Dylan in one of his earlier songs phrased this
great truth: "He who is not busy being born is busy dying." The
Old and the New Testaments describe our failure to live freely
as "participators in God's very own nature" (2 P 1:4).

> I will make the blind walk along the road
>   and lead them along paths.
> I will turn darkness into light before them
>   and rocky places into level tracks.
> ...Listen, you deaf!
> Look and see, you blind! (Is 42:16-18)

We see and yet we do not see. We see beautiful flowers and
fail to see the beautiful face of God shining through the flowers.
We see women and men, as the blind man of Bethsaida
confessed, as "trees walking" (Mk 8:24). We encounter God's

loving presence in our lives each day, at each moment, but we
fail to see him. We are invaded constantly by God's energizing
love in each event. Yet most of us are asleep to that presence.
Jesus still shouts out to us: "Why are you sleeping? Wake up!"
(Lk 22:46).

Ernst Käsemann, the outstanding New Testament
authority, characterizes how most of us fear God's given gift of
freedom and how Church leaders often panic for fear that we
might get carried away by our exercise of such Spirit-freedom:

> What gives most trouble to Christians of all epochs
> is neither lack of faith nor excess of criticism; it is
> Jesus himself, who bestows freedom so open-
> handedly and dangerously on those who do not
> know what to do with it. The Church always gets
> panic-stricken for fear of the turmoil that Jesus
> creates when he comes on the scene; and so it takes
> his freedom under its own management for the
> protection of the souls entrusted to it, in order to
> dispense it in homeopathic doses where it seems
> necessary. They are allowed to possess this freedom
> in the form of hopes and feeling, but only in
> exceptional times may it be turned into action and
> vehemence as otherwise it would blow up the
> Church's structure.[1]

Seeking Freedom

Jesus continually whispers in the hearts of those who are
open to his freedom power, "My truth will make you free" (Jn
8:32). We all eagerly seek freedom. But for many of us freedom
means being able to choose from among two or more
alternatives, with no imposition placed upon us from outside

agents. We speak of a person who is free in business, meaning he answers only to himself and works as he wishes. Sexual freedom usually means no restraints. This applies also to economic and political freedom. Yet enjoying no restraints and no laws actually often inhibits the freedom of others. A person who refuses to accept any restraints is living under the illusion that he is answerable only to himself. Such persons gradually lose true freedom, they become more enslaved to their false ego, their "unspiritual self" (Rm 7:23-24).

True Freedom and the Kingdom of God

Jesus rarely spoke about freedom as such. His role on earth was to be the freeing power of God's love come among all human beings. He preached the good news about the in-breaking of the Father's eternal love as synonymous with his very own person. He knew one did not enjoy freedom by hearing a conference about it or reading a book. People become free by accepting him and his outpoured Spirit of love. Then they would experience that they now really belonged to God's family as his own beloved children, "heirs of God and coheirs with Christ" (Rm 8:15).

Jesus preached about the Kingdom of God, of the Father's passionate love for his children. But he came also to actualize this love of God for all human beings by being a perfect image in human form of the Father's love. The good news that made the captives free from their anxieties and fears was not only that God was a loving Father of infinite mercy, forgiving all human persons who sought his forgiveness, but that he had sent his Son to bring his healing love to the lonely and desolate, hope to the hopeless. Jesus also offered the freeing power of God's Holy Spirit to all who asked the Father for it (Lk 11:13).

It was not so much the words he preached that burst the

bonds that held the human race in slavery, but it was he himself, the Word, who was the liberating power offered to any who would yield to his very person:

> If you make my word your home
> you will indeed be my disciples,
> you will learn the truth
> and the truth will make you free. (Jn 8:31-32)

Those who would enter into the Kingdom of God would have to turn away from all self-absorption in order to turn completely and freely to God. It was not in new rituals, nor in the faithful observance of the externals of the Judaic Law that the freedom of Jesus consisted, but rather in an inner transformation of the heart. Jesus preached such a conversion *(metanoia* in Greek) as the necessary step to true human freedom. Negatively this liberation process was to begin by moving away from the loneliness, alienation and isolation, the state of "unloveliness" and enslavement into which sin had cast the human race, and positively to let God be the complete center of one's life.

Born from Above

But this enlightenment could come only from God's Spirit by way of a new birth. The poor in spirit, who, like children, opened themselves to receive God's Word, Jesus Christ, were able to enter into the Kingdom, which for Jesus was the same as becoming truly free.

True freedom can never be "thingified" into a formula or twelve steps. It is a journey away from our alienation and fragmentation toward an authentic, new life. True and full freedom can only come from the healing power of God made man through the divine Holy Spirit.

Jesus: The Way, the Truth and the Life

Jesus freely entered into our sinful world, like us in all things but sin (Heb 4:15). He saw human beings enslaved to sin and death and "to the elemental principles of this world" (Gal 4:3). His heart, a heart "nearest to the Father's heart" (Jn 1:18), went out to the broken ones who were like sheep without a shepherd (Mt 9:36). When he looked upon the maimed, the blind, the lepers and the paralytics, the epileptics and the possessed, the sinners bound by hatred for others, by lust and pride, he could not but be compassionate, full of mercy and loving as his Father is. Faced with the power of darkness and sin and death, Jesus burned with zeal to bring the light of God's love to destroy their effects.

Jesus Comes To Free the Whole Person

Jesus came to free the whole person, body, soul and spirit. He came to give us life that we might have it more abundantly (Jn 10:10). His love, which was an exact image in human form of the love of the Father for all his human children, was given to each and every person whom he met in his earthly life. He looked into their eyes and poured out a love of infinite power and healing that, to those who believed and accepted it, brought them to a new level of existence and a new found sense of their unique personhood.

Jesus imaged the Father's love most perfectly for all of us when, in the utter silence of his final hour on the cross, he emptied himself out of love to the very last drop of water and of blood. As a result, Jesus loves us in an eternal *now*. St. Paul understood this truth which changed his whole life from Saul the persecutor of the early followers of Christ to Paul, the most ardent and zealous apostle and martyr: "He loved me and sacrificed himself for my sake" (Gal 2:20).

Sin: A Bias toward Ourselves

If we reflect sincerely and humbly upon our daily life we should have a "holy disgust" for the lack of true freedom in our life. Our false ego tells us we are independent. We need no one else. Sin is the thinking and acting out of such a perception. It is a "bias toward self." We feel we must take our lives in hand and determine for ourselves our ultimate direction. Our judgments are made in an attempt to keep alive such an illusion that we need no one. Ultimately sin is the rejection of love, which is a humble movement toward another to give ourselves to the other instead of holding on fiercely in false self-possession of our life.

In such a state we desperately seek to be loved by God and neighbor. Yet our self-absorption resorts to power and attack in order to retain the original perception of our independence from all others. The words of the lawyer in Albert Camus' *The Fall,* become our own:

> Fortunately I arrived! I am the end and the
> beginning; I announce the law. In short, I am a
> judge-penitent.... Ah, *mon ami,* do you know what
> the solitary creature is like as he wanders in big
> cities?[2]

With St. Paul we confess that sin in our members has control over us. Wretches that we are, we can be saved only by God's power in Christ Jesus (Rm 7:24). Our strength is in Jesus Christ, who alone can save us from our alienated self and lead us into the true persons we were destined to be in him.

> ...but if anyone should sin,
> we have our advocate with the Father,
> Jesus Christ, who is just;

He is the sacrifice that takes our sins away,
        and not only ours,
        but the whole world's. (1 Jn 2:1-2)

Free To Love

Jesus and his Holy Spirit bring us into true filial freedom by teaching us the honor and dignity that is ours when we love and obediently serve God. No longer are we concerned to serve our selfish interests, but like Jesus, as Paul tells us, we rather think of the needs of our weak neighbors. "Christ did not think of himself" (Rm 15:3).

In the cross of Christ freedom is revealed as a gift. The Christian under the Spirit of Jesus understands that slavery to egoism is destroyed by Jesus' great personal love for each of us individually. And true freedom is now revealed as God's love in us bringing us into a new kind of slavery. We now belong totally to Jesus Christ. How beautifully Paul experienced in his conversion that true freedom was total surrender to Jesus as Lord. As Jesus is the servant who always says, "Yes" to his Father, so Paul and other Christians are to pass over from their slavery to selfishness, sin, death, the law and the elements of this world that kept the entire cosmos held in bondage (Gal 4:3) into loving service to Jesus Christ.[3]

Paul, after his conversion, saw his freedom in being dead to sin and alive to God in Christ Jesus (Rm 6:10-11). He was now "in Christ," Paul's favorite phrase (he uses it some 164 times to indicate his very real, intimate union with Christ).[4] Christ is now the directing force in Paul's life (Gal 2:20). Paul knew himself to be no longer a slave, but a true son of God, because of the Spirit of Jesus in his heart:

The proof that you are sons is that God has sent the
Spirit of his Son into our hearts: the Spirit that cries,

"Abba, Father," and it is this that makes you a son,
you are not a slave any more; and if God has made
you son, then he has made you heir. (Gal 4:6-7)

A New Creation in Christ

With Paul, all of us Christians share in Christ's own life,
who now gloriously is risen and lives within us. Yet he must be
further formed within us (Gal 4:19). The new freedom he
imparts is one of service, of living, not only as Jesus lived, but
living in union with Jesus through the loving power of the
Spirit of Jesus whom he constantly releases within our hearts.
By yielding to the life-giving presence of Jesus, we Christians
move from freedom to greater freedom by gradually being
more transformed into the "likeness" of Jesus. This is the
eternal destiny that God had planned for us before all ages
(Eph 1:4-7).

In Christ we now are formed into a *new creation* (2 Cor
5:17). The old person is now dead and we are alive to Christ,
who calls us to service in reconciling the whole world to the
Father (2 Cor 5:18-19). Christ's life within us, that begins as an
embryo in Baptism, is to grow as we cooperate with Christ
until we "come to unity in our faith and in our knowledge of
the Son of God, until we become the perfect man, fully mature
with the fullness of Christ himself" (Eph 4:13).

The degree of our growth in true freedom is to be
measured by how completely we make Christ the center of all
our thoughts, words and actions. Everything in us, the values
that we choose to live and act by, must be brought under
obedience to Christ Jesus (2 Cor 10:5). We are to walk in a new
life with Jesus Christ (Rm 6:4). The following chapter will
show how the Spirit leads us into ever growing freedom.

"Where the Spirit of the Lord is, there is freedom" (2 Cor 3:17).
Let us examine some of the areas of our lives where Jesus frees
us from any and all obstacles to the life of Christ within us.

Freedom from the Law

Jesus came not to destroy the Law, but to fulfill it. The
essence of the Law was to love God with all our strength and to
love our neighbors as we love ourselves. When Paul speaks of
the new freedom that Jesus came to give us through his Spirit, he
speaks of the freedom from the Jewish Law:

> Before faith came, we were allowed no freedom by the
> Law; we were being looked after till faith was
> revealed. The Law was to be our guardian until the
> Christ came and we could be justified by faith. Now
> that that time has come, we are no longer under that
> guardian, and you are, all of you, sons and daughters
> of God through faith in Christ Jesus. All baptized in
> Christ, you have all clothed yourselves in Christ, and
> there are no more distinctions between Jew and
> Greek, slave and free, male and female, but all of you
> are one in Christ Jesus. (Gal 3:23-28)

The Purpose of the Law

The purpose of the Law was to hold the Israelites together
in a disciplined unity. It was "a beneficent bondage," in the
words of George Montague.[5] When the child has come of age,
there is no longer need for the slave-servant to accompany him
to school. Jesus Christ has made us sons and daughters of the
heavenly Father (Jn 1:12). We have been given freedom from
the Law only that we might live more fully that for which the

Law was intended, namely, to love God above all things and our neighbor as ourselves through the power of Jesus' Spirit:

> ...the law of the spirit of life in Christ Jesus has set you free from the law of sin and death. God has done what the Law, because of our unspiritual nature, was unable to do. God dealt with sin by sending his own Son in a body as physical as any sinful body, and in that body God condemned sin. (Rm 8:1-3)

Paul insisted that if persons are led by the Holy Spirit, "no law can touch you" (Gal 5:18). The reason for this is that the Spirit abounds in our hearts and can effect infinitely more than the Law ever could have since the Spirit helps us to "carry each other's troubles and fulfill the law of Christ" (Gal 6:2). The commandment that Jesus gives us is to love one another as he has loved us (Jn 15:12).[6]

Jesus Frees Us from Our Religious Idols

Under the rubric of religious idols, we can see how Jesus frees us from having strange gods before the only, true Godhead. Nicholas Berdyaev and Paul Tillich have both articulated for modern readers the contrasting forms of spirituality or religious cultures that they call *heteronomy, autonomy* and *theonomy*.[7] *Nomos* is the Greek word for *law*. *Heteros* in Greek means: the other or some agency outside of the person being affected by any form of authority. It defines a religious attitude that places authority outside of the interiorized, spiritual powers of the individual, informed by the Holy Spirit and relying upon an extrinsic force to constitute the ultimate authority and guarantor of human development.

This can be the religious level of a child incapable for the

time being of a higher transcendence than the authority of
parents, teachers, priests or ministers. For adults, who do not
move into a deeper level of spiritual development, the extrinsic
authority may be some religious leaders, the Bible or other
religious writings given a sacredness through tradition or some
external rituals.

The intrinsic evil when religion becomes heteronomous is
that such persons are shackled into a slavery to some extrinsic
force, taking away from them the necessity to evolve further by
being open to the Spirit. Tillich bluntly defines it as *demonic*.
"For the demonic is something finite, something limited, which
puts on infinite, unlimited dignity."[8] We have all met
"religious" persons who hide behind the demanding authority of
a teaching body of bishops or the Bible in a fundamentalist way,
kosher food practices, Koran injunctions, extreme devotions of a
magical superstitious type to saints, relics or certain ritual
practices. These can never be ultimates in themselves. They
must be inserted into a higher level of self-direction. The Spirit
of the risen Savior frees us from any idolatry of forms and allows
us to put all such structures of extrinsic authority into a
synthesis permeated by the Spirit's guidance.

Autonomy

As children grow into adolescence they break away from
the dominant authority of their parents to enjoy greater
individual freedom and self-determination. Adults on a religious
level and even whole churches can likewise move from a
heteronomous to an autonomous level of being. Tillich defines
autonomous culture as "the attempt to create the forms of
personal and social life without any reference to something
ultimate and unconditional, following only the demands of
theoretical and practical rationality."[9]

The main characteristic of such autonomy is that we ourselves become the center, determining our values without any outside authority and without any other transcendent values except our own inner preferences as we see all things in reference to ourselves as the ultimate criterion of what is good and true. Basically this is a reaction against an older type of religion or spirituality, but it only serves to keep us enslaved.

Jesus frees us from a "me-ism" that enslaves us to our own intellectual and volitional powers as the ultimate criterion of what is truly right and pleasing to God.

Theonomy

Theonomy is a spirituality in which we place ourselves under the interior presence of the Holy Spirit, operating, as Tillich calls it, as the divine ground of our being that lies at the depth of reason. Literally *theonomy* comes from the Greek, *theos,* meaning God and *nomos,* meaning *law.* Such a religious approach is able to inform the heteronomous forms and those of the autonomous with true meaning since theonomy is rooted in the ultimacy of God himself, directly and immediately.

Theonomy is rooted in the spiritual presence of God as holy, both within ourselves and within every atom of the universe. One is in touch with the "uncreated energies" of God's loving activities throughout the entire universe, but especially within the lives of individuals. Theonomy is the meeting of our inspirited being and God's Spirit in loving communication (Rm 8:15). Theonomy is rooted in faith, hope and love whereby we can be in touch with God Trinity in the most personalistic and loving way in each moment of time.

Theonomy is a "meta-rational" way of coming to "see" God and to "hear" him. It is the burgeoning forth of the Spirit manifested by the loving surrender of ourselves into his loving care as we strive with all our might to fulfill the God-given potential within us. Theonomy is the fulfillment of the image and likeness of God within us. It is an ongoing process of the "in-breaking" of God into our history that is fashioned by our *praxis*, the disciplining of ourselves away from any self-centeredness, that tends to make us fall back into a heteronomous or autonomous way of operating.

This penetrating into the "insideness" of things Tillich is fond of calling the "depth-dimension." This is the freeing power of the Holy Spirit that allows theonomy to keep religion from becoming an idol. Tillich defines this dimension: "...the religious aspect points to that which is ultimate, infinite, unconditioned in one's spiritual life."[10]

Freedom from Death and the Powers of This World

Jesus sets us free from the corruptible which, in Paul's vision, is the absence of God's eternal life living in us. The risen Lord has come to bring us life and that more abundantly (Jn 10:10). With faith in the conquering power of the risen Jesus within our lives, we have already passed beyond the stage of living only a temporal, material existence. Jesus constantly speaks to us: "I was dead and now I am to live forever and ever, and I hold the keys of death and of the underworld" (Rv 1:18). Therefore, because "...Jesus was put to death for our sins and raised to life to justify us" (Rm 4:25), death has no sting, no victory" (1 Cor 15:55) over us. We now live in eternal life, even as we still journey on this earth.

The Greatest Death Is to Selfishness

Because we have died the greatest death to selfishness and now live unto Christ, we truly have been set free of our greatest fear, the fear of death. We dread death because it is a threat to our meaningfulness. We have been made by God to live with purpose, to praise, reverence and serve the Triune God. The idea of this being frustrated by physical death causes us great fear and sadness. But through our faith, hope and love, the Spirit of the risen Jesus makes it possible for us to live already in the new time (*kairos*), the time of salvation and ever increasing freedom. It is his perfect love that drives out all fear (1 Jn 4:18).

Freedom from Cares

Jesus came to free us from all excessive anxiety and fear that come from being overly solicitous in our insecurity. This is part of the consistent message that he preached:

> But you, you must not set your hearts on things to
> eat and drink; nor must you worry.... Your Father
> well knows you need these things. No; set your
> hearts on his kingdom, and these other things will be
> given you as well. There is no need to be afraid, little
> flock, for it has pleased your Father to give you the
> kingdom. (Lk 12:22-32)

According to the teaching of Jesus the primary focus of all our striving in our earthly life must be on the heavenly Father. This was how he lived. He releases his Holy Spirit so that in all of the events in each and every moment of our lives we can, in the Spirit, cry out, "Abba, Father!" (Rm 8:15). Everything: the

world, life and death, the present and the future are all our
servants, "but you belong to Christ and Christ belongs to God"
(1 Cor 3:23).

Fear Not

One of the greatest psychic enslavements is fear. It is the
opposite of faith which is a gift of God's Spirit of love. When
we lack the healing experience of God's personal love for us, we
lack a sense of true identity. Fear is primarily centered in the
apprehension of a future danger, unhappiness, doubt, anxiety,
worry, dread, hatred, anger, horror, fright or terror. The
thought of such impending evil weighs heavily upon our psyche
and our body, crippling our growth, breaking down our health.

Fear can be about countless objects. It is the state of fear
from which we must be delivered, for often the objects that we
fear are only in our minds. The nation's number one health
problem lies in the area, not so much of bodily disease, but of
emotional and mental illness. And most of these psychic
disturbances are due to needless fear. At one time or another
most doctors are confronted with trying to heal the effects of
fear. But to do so effectively they must get at the root of fear
which is often centered in a lack of faith and trust in God's
loving care for us.

How often Jesus spoke words of confidence and loving
strength to those burdened with fear. To the frightened
disciples behind locked doors in the Upper Room after his
death, he uttered these fear-dissolving words: "Peace be with
you!... Why are you so agitated, and why are these doubts
rising in your hearts?" (Lk 24:37-38). We say, "Yes, Lord, I
believe," yet we begin all over to fear new areas of the unknown.
This cripples us and prevents us from living free, dynamic and

decisive lives. We wait for others to decide things for us, and we lose the freedom to determine our lives in God's grace.

We become liberated from the bondage of fear when we begin to look at fear itself in terms not only of our own strength, but also the strength of God. Are we ready and willing to let go of these fears that allow us an enslaving "comfort" and security instead of our pushing into a true, dying process that many of us are not quite ready to make due to our weak faith, hope and love in the Trinity's great love for us?

A Paschal Freedom

Through his resurrection, Jesus is able to touch us in our confining fears and petty slaveries and to lead us into true freedom. It is his Spirit, who alone can lead us "to know Christ and the power of his resurrection and to share his sufferings by reproducing the pattern of his death. That is the way I can hope to take my place in the resurrection of the dead" (Ph 3:10-12). We are free to the extent that we are willing to surrender to the Spirit of the risen Lord and to live in his freeing power.

Jesus' Holy Spirit is God's gift of love and freedom. Let us now see how the Holy Spirit brings us true freedom as we are "divinized" and become "new creatures" in Christ Jesus (2 Cor 5:17).

Chapter Six

The Freeing Power of the Spirit

Nicholas Berdyaev, the twentieth-century Russian philosopher, describes true freedom as a victory in the area of the spiritual world:

> Victory, not only over the fear of death, but over death itself, is the realization of personality. The realization of personality is impossible in the finite. It presupposes the infinite, not quantitative infinity, but qualitative, i.e., eternity. The individual person dies, since he is born in the generic process, but personality does not die, since it is not born in the generic process.
>
> Victory over the fear of death is the victory of spiritual personality over the biological individual. But this does not mean the separation of the immortal spiritual principle from the mortal human principle, but the transfiguration of the whole person. Freedom must be loving and love must be free. It is only the gathering together of freedom, truth and love, which realizes personality, free and creative personality. We pass from slavery to freedom, from a state of disintegration to a condition of completeness, from impersonality to personality,

from passivity to creativeness, that is to say, he
passes over to spirituality.[1]

True freedom cannot be realized outside of the process of
continued integration of all levels of our human being under the
dynamic action of God's Love, who in Scripture is called the
Holy Spirit. St. Paul taught that where there is the Spirit of God
there is true liberty (2 Cor 3:18). The majority of us human
beings are not free, but we are held captive by our dark side, our
false ego. We live in a constant fear of life and of death. By
refusing to live at the center of our whole being, body, soul and
spirit (1 Th 5:23), we are barraged constantly by fearful thoughts
of our unworthiness, of sin and death.

We are not integrated persons. We feel worthless and live
meaningless lives.

St. Paul describes what our integration and our authentic
holiness should consist of:

> May the God of peace make you perfect and holy;
> and may you all be kept safe and blameless, spirit,
> soul and body, for the coming of our Lord Jesus
> Christ. (1 Th 5:23)

What Is Our Spirit?

It should be relatively easy for all of us to understand that
we are made up of body and soul. To understand the concept of
our human *spirit* where true freedom and full integration take
place, we must go to the Holy Spirit. We will discover that the
human spirit cannot be considered as a static part of our
humanity. Our human spirit in Scripture is seen as our
personhood in our unique personality in vital communication
with God.

Neshamah in Hebrew means "breath" and describes life as found both in God and in us human beings.[2] "Then he breathed into his nostrils a breath of life, and thus man became a living being" (Gn 2:7).

The Hebrew word, *ruah* or *ruach,* is the usual term in the Old Testament for "wind" or "spirit," to indicate God's presence among his human creatures and all of his creation. It often connotes a presence of God by *power.* If God's spirit is operating throughout all of nature, fashioning both human beings and all other creatures in a mysterious, awesome way, his Spirit is more powerfully operating in his condescending, *hesed,* covenantal love for his people. God's Spirit comes upon individuals and his entire people to restore them to new, love relationships with him.

God is most *spirit* when he is renewing his people by giving them "a new heart." God breathes his love into his chosen people. Repentance opens his people up to receive his breathing-in Spirit of Love enabling them to become alive again by sharing life-giving relationships with Yahweh.

> I shall give you a new heart, and put a new spirit in you; I shall remove the heart of stone from your bodies and give you a heart of flesh instead. I shall put my spirit in you and make you keep my laws and sincerely respect my observances.... You shall be my people and I will be your God. (Ezk 36:26-28)

God's spirit, in Isaiah's prophecy, is to come upon the Servant of the Lord: "I have endowed him with my spirit that he may bring true justice to the nations" (Is 42:1). The same Servant confesses: "The spirit of the Lord Yahweh has been given to me, for Yahweh has anointed me" (Is 61:1).

The Spirit of Jesus

In the New Testament the Spirit of God relates to Jesus in two distinct ways. In the most common manner in the Synoptic Gospels, the Spirit has priority, comes upon Jesus and anoints him. Jesus is first conceived by the power of God's Spirit, is baptized and anointed for his mission by the Spirit. Jesus is driven into the desert by the Holy Spirit. He casts out demons by the Spirit's power. He heals and performs all sorts of miracles in the same Spirit-power (Ac 10:38).

Jesus Sends the Holy Spirit

In the Pauline and Johannine writings we find the second manner of the Spirit's relating to Jesus. Not only does Jesus *receive* the Spirit, but he *sends* the Holy Spirit upon his followers. The Spirit is the Spirit of Christ or of the Son (Rm 8:9; 2 Cor 3:17; Gal 4:6; Ph 1:19). Jesus promises: "I will send him (the Advocate) to you" (Jn 16:7).

Jesus could not give the Spirit until he had died (Jn 7:39). He had first to receive God's Spirit before he could share him with others. He, who was the image of the Father, first had to receive in his human life the immense love of God. Then he, dying by the power of so great a love for us, could release that same love within our hearts.

In order to understand more clearly the *freeing* power of the Holy Spirit, let us see that God's Spirit is more than an instrument that Jesus sends into our lives to perfect his people. With this aspect we are all familiar. Without a doubt it is rooted in Scripture. Jesus sends us the Spirit to complete his work on earth (Jn 14:26). The Holy Spirit brings us into true filiation as children of God (Rm 8:15; Gal 4:6). This is the fulfillment of one of the roles of God's Spirit in Holy Scripture.

The Holy Spirit Is a Creative Force

The Holy Spirit is a creative force that is new and distinct from Jesus. He is a special, loving power, different from the special, loving power of Jesus. Yet he is also associated with the risen Christ. "We know that he lives in us by the Spirit that he has given us" (1 Jn 3:24). Traditionally we tend to look upon the Spirit as the one who opens us up to Jesus Christ and his redeeming power on the cross.[3] But the New Testament presents the Holy Spirit in a different way. Jesus died, but now he lives!

The Holy Spirit is presented as the avenue through which the risen Jesus exists and acts in the world. Jesus is the new Adam. He is the first fruits, the first-born of many sons. Risen, Jesus is what the whole world is to become. The work of the Spirit is to be Christ's life-giving Spirit to the world. He draws us into Christ, into his Body. He divinizes us, making us "new creatures" in Christ Jesus (2 Cor 5:17).

A Life-Giving Spirit

God the Father showed his acceptance of the sacrifice of Jesus by exalting him through the resurrection. In the resurrection Christ, the perfect man, passed over from the condition of flesh *(sarx),* which was subject to death into the new condition of *spirit (pneuma)* and now becomes the life-giving Spirit, the Head of the new humanity, established by him as the new people of God through his Spirit.

In Christ's death, God condemned sin in the flesh (Rm 8:3). The power of sin and death was broken. The resurrection of Christ is uniquely important because his new and glorious life makes him the New Adam and the Lord of the Universe, capable now in his exalted existence in glory of bestowing upon

us the same life of the Spirit by making us children of his
heavenly Father.

Jesus insisted that it was imperative that he leave his
disciples because, if he did not go, the Advocate would not
come to them (Jn 16:7). When his whole being is glorified by
the Father's Spirit, it becomes for all of us the source of the
Spirit, of eternal life. Now Jesus risen cannot be separated from
his Spirit. The Spirit is God's life-giving "Breath" that the risen
Jesus is always breathing upon us. We can see why St. John tells
us that Jesus could not have given his Spirit before he had died
(Jn 7:39).

Body, Soul and Spirit

We cannot understand our slavery to sin and death or our
ultimate dignity to which God has called us as free children of
the heavenly Father until we see our destiny from all eternity as
being, by Jesus' Spirit, "in Christ."

The early Greek Fathers built a theological anthropology
around the biblical model of image and likeness. Simply put,
from the teachings of the first great Christian theologian, St.
Irenaeus of the second century, all human beings have been
made by God to live "according to the image of God," that is
Jesus Christ. We are made in a basic "image" of God and are
called to move into a relationship of dynamic "likeness."[5]

Before our baptism into Christ, we possessed body and
soul relations. God's "breath" in us as embodied beings (soma
in Greek) allows us to relate as a whole being, a psycho-physical
unity, a personality ad extra, in relation to the created, material
world around us. As "embodied-persons," we also have soul
relations, the psyche with all the emotions and passions along
with the intellectual and volitional life that allows us to relate to
other "ensouled beings."

The Meaning of Spirit in Us

For Irenaeus and the majority of the early Eastern Fathers, *spirit* is not yet in human beings who are born into sin and death and do not have God's deeper life in them. We do not yet possess according to Irenaeus the *likeness* to Jesus Christ. This means that this state of living in God's grace through the Holy Spirit of the risen Jesus is not possible since it is only the Holy Spirit of the risen Lord who can bring us into this friendship with the indwelling Trinity. We must cooperate as adults in order to come into such "spirit-relationships" with the Trinity through fully conscious and willed acts of faith, hope and love.

Let us quote from St. Irenaeus his important insight into the full meaning of what it means for a Christian to be an "inspirited" being:

> Now the soul and the spirit are certainly a part of the human person but certainly are not the whole person. For the perfect person consists in the commingling and the union of the soul, receiving the Spirit of the Father and the admixture of that fleshly nature, which was molded after the image of God.
>
> But when the spirit here blended with the soul is united to God's handiwork, the person is rendered spiritual and perfect because of the outpouring of the Spirit, and this is he who was made in the image and likeness of God. But if the Spirit be wanting to the soul, he who is such is indeed of an animal nature, and being left carnal, shall be an imperfect being, possessing indeed the image of God in his formation, but not receiving the likeness through the Spirit and thus in this being imperfect.... Those

> then are the perfect, who have had the Spirit of God
> remaining in them, and have preserved their souls
> and bodies blameless, holding fast the faith of God,
> that is, that faith which is directed toward God and
> maintaining righteous dealings with respect to their
> neighbors.[6]

Thus from a biblical, theological point of view, we human beings are incomplete and imperfect until we enter into an integration of body-soul-spirit relations with ourselves, the material world around us, loving union with other human beings and ultimately with God. Now we can see that the Spirit of Jesus is God's breathing into us of his very own loving energies, drawing us ever more through the events of each day (the historical perspective) into a deeper, ontological relationship with the risen Lord Jesus. This has been the plan that God has had for all of us from all eternity (Eph 1:4-8).

The Spirit Regenerates

We are brought into a new creation through Baptism. It is this initiation sacrament that brings us into direct contact with the resurrected, glorified Christ through the life-giving Spirit. St. Paul writes to Titus:

> It was for no reason except his own compassion that
> he saved us, by means of the cleansing water of
> rebirth and by renewing us with the Holy Spirit
> which he has so generously poured over us through
> Jesus Christ, our Savior. He did this so that we
> should be justified by his grace, to become heirs
> looking forward to inheriting eternal life. (Tt 3:4-7)

The Spirit of Jesus risen dwells within us, making our very bodies temples of God (1 Cor 3:16; 1 Cor 6:19). The Spirit brings us into direct contact with the spiritualized Body-Person of Jesus risen who dwells also within us along with the indwelling heavenly Father whom Jesus promised would come with him to dwell within us as in a mansion (Jn 14:23).

True Regeneration Is a Freeing Process

True regeneration brought about by the Holy Spirit is a freeing process, a true liberation. No longer is the Christian bound by darkness and illusion. We can become enlightened by the light of God's indwelling presence to know the truth, that we are in Christ, sharing in his risen life. We are truly children of the Father (Jn 1:13; Jn 3:3, 5, 7).

The freeing power of the Holy Spirit, therefore, consists primarily in an ongoing process of leading us out of slavery from sin and death and the Law into true liberty as children of God. As the Spirit reveals to us daily the resurrectional power of Jesus' presence within us, allowing us to live each moment in him and with him, we learn to accept our true identity. Living in the present *now,* we can live in the unchangeable, eternal *now* of God's love for us in Christ Jesus. This is not a mere static, Platonic *idea* that we reach by an illumination to discover what was always true — God's perfect love for us from all eternity.

The Holy Spirit progressively effects our regeneration into children of God as we yield to his power in us. The Spirit has liberated us from the slavery of sin (Rm 6:17). We have truly been reborn from above, not merely by water, but by the Holy Spirit (Jn 3:5). Yet with St. Paul we can confess that we are prisoners "of that law of sin which lives inside my body" (Rm 7:23).

Yet the Good News is that my rebirth is always taking place at this moment that the Spirit pushes me to live according to my inner dignity of being in Christ, a part of his Body, a child of God.

Life in the Holy Spirit

Paul assigns to the Holy Spirit the character, initiative and salvific action proper to a person. Through personal experience "in the Spirit," he had discovered the world of the Spirit. It was for him a "new sphere of life" (Rm 6:4). The work of the Spirit is to create this new life of the risen Christ in the individual Christian. As we become alive by the Spirit, so Paul would exhort us then that we must walk by the Spirit (Gal 5:16, 26). Christians are to be *pneumatikoi*, i.e., spiritualized by the Spirit, since the primary function of the Spirit is to create this life in Christ. Paul sees the world tied together in a hope of being set free from its slavery to decadence in order "to enjoy the same freedom and glory as the children of God" (Rm 8:20-21).

We do not possess the fullness of the Spirit but we have come into the "first-fruits of the Spirit" (Rm 8:23). Still we have the pledge and guarantee of its completion (2 Cor 1:22; Eph 1:14). Thus we can see that for Paul the phrases "in the Spirit" and "in Christ" complement one another.

Guided by the Holy Spirit

The Spirit is given in embryonic form in Baptism to bring about the fullness of Christ's life by making us conform gradually through progressive growth to a greater likeness to Christ. This life in the Spirit will have an eschatological fruition in the life to come: "…but if Christ is in you, then your spirit is life itself because you have been justified; and if the Spirit of him who raised Jesus from the dead is living in you, then he who raised Jesus from the dead will give life to your own mortal bodies through his Spirit living in you" (Rm 8:9-11).

We Christians are caught between two forces: the power of evil and the Spirit of Christ, between the unspiritual in us and the spiritual. We are to live according to the Spirit, who is the new principle of Christ-like operations within us. The Spirit creates this new life in Christ living within us. He fosters it, stimulates its growth, purifies us from any obstacles to its maturity. He brings this life to its fullness in the proportion that we allow this Spirit to be the normative influence guiding us in all our moral choices that determine our true growth in Christ and give us our true uniqueness.

Ideally, the life of a Christian should be a "spiritual" one, a turning within, to be guided by the Spirit. No longer is there an extrinsic code of morality, a Judaic Law or any other law operating exclusively as our sole guide. Idols constructed by human beings come crashing down as the Christian gives the Spirit full freedom to work within his or her human context. Paul writes:

> [I]f you are guided by the Spirit, you will be in no danger of yielding to self-indulgence, since self-indulgence is the opposite of the Spirit, the Spirit is totally against such a thing.... If you are led by the Spirit, no law can touch you.... What the Spirit brings is very different: love, joy, peace, patience, kindness, goodness, trustfulness, gentleness and self-control. There can be no law against things like that, of course. You cannot belong to Christ Jesus unless you crucify all self-indulgent passions and desires. Since the Spirit is our life, let us be directed by the Spirit. (Gal 5:16-25)

Christian Morality

We are to listen attentively under the guidance of the Holy Spirit to the living Word within us. The Spirit reveals to us God's will through the fabric of our daily life, our family, our larger community, the Church, the whole human race. In particular it means to respond to the living Word within us through the illumination of the Holy Spirit. Thus we seek the norm for right conduct, which can never be merely an extrinsic law or our own rational way of guiding our conduct. This becomes a response to the living Word in us, a response to the Holy Spirit speaking also within the Church through Tradition and the teaching body empowered by the same Spirit of Jesus to teach us without error.

Finally it is a response to the union with others experienced in the Eucharist which becomes the paradigm of our larger union with all human beings. Jesus did not give us a highly involved moral system. Paul and the other New Testament writers also did not want to present us with another Law written in stone. We are under a new law: "The law of the Spirit of life in Christ Jesus has set you free from the law of sin and death" (Rm 8:2). Charity or agape is the touchstone to the law of the Spirit. It was divine love that moved God to send us his Son. That same love is powerful enough in us to uproot inordinate self-love which holds us in slavery.

Love of Neighbor

True freedom is self-determination in the inmost depths of our being. It is opposed, as has been pointed out in previous chapters, to every kind of external determination, which is a force or compulsion from without or from within. We enter into true self-determination only when, in the depths of our being, we touch God's Spirit, who releases our spirit to become a loving movement in freedom toward others. True self-determination and self-giving love to others become synonymous and are the freeing work of the Holy Spirit. The fruit of the Spirit is love (Gal 5:22).

And the basis for true love for other human beings is always the love of God that is experienced within our inner spirit or our heart. This is not only the work of the Holy Spirit. This ultimately is what the Holy Spirit is. He is the applied love of the crucified Jesus, the image of Jesus, now risen and living within us by the indwelling Spirit. Jesus is one with the heavenly Father, living within us and loving us in that eternal, unchanging love.

In prayer the Spirit comes to our spirit, namely, our whole being in openness to the Spirit of God to be guided as to how best we can love God with our whole heart and love our neighbor as ourselves. The Spirit bears witness to our spirit that we are truly loved as the Father loves his eternal Son (Rm 8:15). God's very own dynamic current of love, between Father and Son, catches us up and regenerates us into new creatures, ever-more consciously aware of our inner dignity having been so privileged as to be loved infinitely by God.

Living on a New Level of Being

We begin to live on a new level of being. We perceive ourselves in a new light. We walk in that inner dignity, all because of what Jesus Christ and the Spirit have done. "We are God's work of art, created in Christ Jesus to live the good life as from the beginning he had meant us to live it" (Eph 2:10). We perceive other human beings differently. It is not now with our own rational thinking, so often distorted by sin and ignorance of our true being in Christ, that we view others.

We see the same world that we looked upon daily before, but now we see "inside." We see that all others are loved infinitely by God, even though they might not have experienced that same Spirit of love within themselves. We understand now that we really are one with them. They are our brothers and sisters and we are all parts of the Body of Christ. How can we hurt ourselves? How can we judge others who, in their ignorance, do not realize who they really are?

Love now becomes, not something we strive to do. Rather Love is the Spirit of God informing our spirit, the deepest levels of our consciousness, with the unifying force of God's very own uncreated energies. These unite us with God and with our neighbors as we seek to perform every thought, word and deed in the spirit of love. "Whatever you eat, whatever you drink, whatever you do at all, do it for the glory of God" (1 Cor 10:31).

The Greatest Freeing Power of the Spirit

The greatest freeing by the Spirit comes about when we are liberated from the fear and dark anxieties, the aggressive "charging" toward others that lead us to try to control and possess them as "things." We are free when we are able to love each person we meet in the power of God's Spirit. That which is impossible to our human personality becomes possible through the Holy Spirit who fashions us into the likeness of Christ. Rooted in faith, hope and love, we enjoy the free creativity of the Spirit as children of God. In hope we love others in God's eternal love for them which then brings about a freeing in them to become actually what we have loved in the Spirit's hope.

The Spirit is the creative, transforming power of God that is always uniting what is divided. We enter into that same creative power of God to call other persons into their true, transcendent selves in the freedom of the indwelling Spirit. The

same Spirit allows us to let go of our own fashioning of the
world according to our own image and to enter into God's
movement of free creation.

This is the great work of the Holy Spirit. He frees us to
become the true persons God has always known us to be in his
Son, Jesus Christ. He frees us from self-hate and insecurity,
from all fear and anxiety so that we can become the presence of
Jesus in a world that has not yet heard the Good News. The
Spirit of Jesus frees us so that we can enter into eternal peace
and joy, the ultimate fruit of the Spirit's love as we realize more
and more that we are members of Christ. The Spirit's greatest
gift is to make actual for all human beings, in a freeing process
through contemplation, the truth:

> You have stripped off your own behavior with your
> old self, and you have put on a new self which will
> progress toward true knowledge the more it is
> renewed in the image of its Creator; and in that
> Image there is no room for distinction between
> Greek and Jew, between the circumcised or the
> uncircumcised, or between barbarian and Scythian,
> slave and free man. There is only Christ: he is
> everything and he is in everything. (Col 3:9-11)

Chapter Seven

Mysticism and Freedom

All of us no doubt long to be more holy, more loving, more one within ourselves, with God, with all other human beings and with all of God's creatures. We are like lonely pilgrims searching for the fountain of youth that will destroy the death-gnawing elements within us and around us and give us eternal life. We long to become complete, whole, integrated persons who are capable of leading meaningful lives.

But are we ready to go deeper into ourselves? Are we not content with the worlds we have created or have received from the creations of others? Do we not fear losing control over those worlds by pushing our consciousness to deeper levels as we actuate the hidden treasures of our unique personhood locked in the dark abysses of our unconscious?

Dr. Carl G. Jung saw the need for us to know ourselves and the inner working of our psyches. He spoke these words in 1959 on a BBC telecast:

> One thing is sure — a great change of psychological attitude is imminent. That is certain. And why? Because we need more psychology. We need more understanding of human nature, because the only real danger that exists is man himself. He is the real danger, and we are pitifully unaware of it. We know

nothing of man — far too little. His psyche should be
studied, because we are the origin of all coming evil.

Awakening to the World of the Spirit

I believe that for many persons throughout the world we
are beginning to see a great surge toward *mysticism*. Karl
Rahner, the great Catholic theologian, insisted that only those
who experience God will continue to grow as human beings, and
hence as truly religious persons. "The devout Christian of the
future will either be a 'mystic,' one who has 'experienced'
something or he will cease to be anything at all."[1]

The artisan and poet, M.C. Richards, in her book, *The
Crossing Point,* expresses this inner hunger:

> One of the truths of our time is this hunger deep in
> people all over the planet for coming into relationship
> with each other. Human consciousness is crossing a
> threshold as mighty as the one from the Middle Ages
> to the Renaissance. People are hungering and
> thirsting after experience that feels true to them on
> the inside after so much hard work mapping the outer
> spaces of the physical world. They are gaining
> courage to ask for what they need: living inter-
> connections, a sense of individual worth, shared
> opportunities.[2]

Starved for an immediate experience in the deepest reaches
of their consciousness, many Westerners are turning on to the
Absolute Being. In our dehumanized, rationalist world, we are
rich in techniques, poor in intuitions, in feminine receptivity to
the inner voice that resides within us, in the "temple invisible."
Yet we see everywhere the reaction to a technological world that

places supreme value on the laws of the observable as the only index of reality.

Persons are crying out to understand themselves as unique persons discovered in the intimacy of an *I-Thou* loving relationship that will drive away the fearful solitary loneliness of a person reduced to a digit or a statistic.

Decline of Inner Experience

Today our specialists can predict our future or at least we place great trust in their predictions. Science has taken away from us the glow of any astonishment and excitement as we are left with an objective world that follows science's discovered laws. We are afraid to look and see the poetry of soft greens of spring or the wild, macabre dance of trees, intoxicated by an autumn rain storm because our scientists tell us it is a question only of light waves and high pressure points shooting through the nation!

Such stress on objective knowledge has lessened or completely obliterated any experience of the mystery of our inner life with its experience of God's uncreative energies of graceful and healing love. The most fascinating world lies within all of us where the Divine Trinity dwells in loving presence and yet most of us are scarcely aware, beyond an intellectual assent given to a truth revealed by God through his Church, of all this inner richness and beauty. In the words of the poet Gerard Manley Hopkins, "...these things, these things were always there, but for the beholder."[3]

Need of Religion and Depth Psychology

We have insisted that true love and freedom go together. Today modern psychology can be a great help to us, for an understanding both of the working of our psyche and of the "place" where, in inner attentiveness and loving prayer, we can confront our false self and the destructive elements deeply ingrained in our unconscious and find healing and wholeness. But it is also in the unconscious of our psyche that we can experience immediately and directly through God's "numinous" presence, inside of matter and spirit, the distant outline of our true self in our oneness with the Absolute *ONE*.

Consciousness Originates in the Unconscious

Jung gives us a basic principle that consciousness originates in the unconscious. As long as you and I remain strangers to our unconscious, we will remain also strangers to our true self. Anthony Haglof, O.C.D., affirms this Jungian insight: "Jung in fact gives the name of *self* to the totality of psychic factors which must be consciously integrated within the personality for human beings to achieve the goal long ago set for them by Life itself, while the totality of this *self* remains hidden, as seems to be more and more the case with us Westerners because of our inveterate materialism and rationalism. Even in the area of religion, we continue to bask in one illusion after another."[4]

No deeper consciousness of our true self, made by God in Christ's image and likeness, can be attained without a greater complementarity between modern depth psychology and religion. This begins as an interdiscipline between the ancient wisdom and authentic practices of religion and that of modern depth psychology. It is a great grace for us living at this time in human history to come into such a new synthesis.

This does not mean that individuals in times past did not explore the depths of the unconscious and push their habitual level of consciousness to a greater and more intense understanding of what it means to be a human person, "sharers of God's own divine nature" (2 P 1:4). Surely the true mystics down through the centuries stand as those fearless persons, led by the Spirit of God's overshadowing love, who did not fear to push their consciousness to these deeper levels in order to actuate the hidden treasures of their unique personhood locked in the dark abysses of their unconscious.[5]

Primordial Experiences

Dr. Ann Belford Ulanov in her book, *Religion and the Unconscious,* shows that, although depth psychology and Christian theology have different approaches and methodologies, yet "they share a concentration on the hidden depths of human experience and a determination to probe these depths. They go beyond their differences to an intermingling of styles, techniques, and procedures in their common concern with that special kind of human experience which we think is best called *primordial experience.*"[6]

The Presence of God in the Unconscious

Authentic religion has the power to set us free from the cultural coding that permits traditions to become fixed and impersonal. Such "traditional religion" operates solely on the secondary process of directive, conscious thinking and cuts off any true progress, measured by the intensity of our consciousness of God's perfect love present within us and throughout the entire cosmos. True religion allows us to move into the hidden areas of the unconscious to make contact with the genetic coding that is grounded in the numinous and sacred presence of God as Love. This fiery presence of God, the Source of all being, is present within the human unconscious and is locked into the matrix of each atom and subatomic particle. It becomes present, but not as an object to be manipulated by our human consciousness, so basically prone toward self-seeking. Rather, it becomes present as the Creator brings forth through his Logos the uniqueness of the individual person according to God's own image and likeness.

The Map of Our Psyche

One of Carl Jung's commentators, Dr. Ira Progoff, compares the psyche to a cross-sectional drawing of a geological rock formation. At the top is a thin layer of surface rock that we call consciousness. Below this is a thicker layer of rock that we call the personal unconscious. Underlying both of these layers there is a dark, volcanic base extending back to the very core of the earth itself, bringing the individual into primordial contact with all of creation as a part to the whole. This Jung calls the collective unconscious or conscience of the Universal Man. Occasionally out of this volcano there erupt materials that rise to the surface, passing through the other layers.[7]

If we are to attain an integrated personality and authentic freedom to love God with our whole heart and our neighbor as we love our true selves in God's perfect love, we must harmonize all the various levels of our psychic life within our minds. Jung calls this the process of "individuation" which he describes as "the better and more complete fulfillment of the collective qualities of the human being."[8]

What Does Expanded Consciousness Mean?

If Jung's principle is correct that expanded consciousness originates in the unconscious, we must ask ourselves just what is the conscious and the unconscious? With so much discussion today about consciousness expanded to a oneness with God and the entire universe, we need to seek to define its meaning. Is it something that we can acquire by taking a seminar or by reading a self-help book, thus raising our mental and spiritual level of consciousness, so important if we are truly to love God and neighbor authentically in the gift of freedom given to us by the Holy Spirit of Love?

Is it merely a higher state of neural functioning? And, if so, are there techniques to develop such functioning? Or is it an inner light on which we focus in order to see objects in greater detail, as with bifocals, to aid our limited vision? Dr. Arthur Diekman defines consciousness as "awareness," rather than "the things of which we are aware."[9]

It is a mistake to think of consciousness as self-reflection or introspection of some sort. Consciousness is not primarily this ability to "bend back" upon oneself in reflection. It is rather a simple, internal experience of oneself and one's activities of sensing, feeling, thinking, judging, reflecting, deciding and acting.[10] Consciousness is more than to know an object. It is basically not the presence of an object to a subject, but the simple presence in non-reflective awareness of the subject to herself/himself. There are different levels of conscious functioning. Bernard Lonergan, S.J., describes the three basic stages in our "knowing" process, i.e., first, dreaming, then the level of the experience of our five senses, followed by understanding, insight, theory, hypothesis and conceptualization.

Beyond these there occurs the level of reflection, or weighing evidence and judging. But consciousness must not be limited to the level of knowing alone. Beyond the level of knowing there is that of deliberation, feeling, conscious response to values, decision and action. Finally, there is the higher level, the graced level of being in intimate love with

God.[11] This level embraces ordinary conscious, God-inspired love for God. This level embraces also God-inspired acts of faith, hope and love, as well as many mystical experiences that Dr. Roberto Assagioli calls acts of the "Superconscious."[12]

What Is Mysticism?

In all human beings there exists a propensity toward mysticism. We all have within ourselves a universal drive toward union with the Supreme Reality. If we call that Reality God, we are saying that all other finite beings must ultimately fail to satisfy our thirst for deeper, more intense interpenetration with God. All of us have enjoyed perhaps moments of ecstatic human love, a gasp of awe at some breathtaking natural beauty, a lifting of oneself out of our habitual mode of perceiving the real world around us and an entering into a world of seemingly greater simplification while listening to transcendent music.

The mystic is the "seer" of this inner world of ultimate reality who habitually lives on such a level of simplification and union with God. This does not mean that mystics reduce everything to an unreal denomination. Like a child living on a level of intense, sensate impressions, authentic mystics bypass the logical world of labels and concepts to immerse themselves completely in a world of immediate sensations. They hear, see, smell, taste, touch the created world around them with a freedom and innocence as though the experiences were the first they ever had. They drink in all of reality possible from each experience, receiving more than giving, reverencing more than possessively manipulating that reality.

This is only one part, the beginning of the mystical experience: of union with life in any form. The higher activity of mysticism that lifts it to a plane of highest human activity is the union that the mystics perceive in their awareness of being united, both with the object perceived and the ultimate Ground of Being that penetrates both subject and object and brings both into a oneness. Mystics see their own unique individuation in contrast to the rest of reality, yet at the same time their degree of oneness both with God and the real world outside themselves gives them a simplified consciousness of *becoming* one with the whole of reality.

Mysticism Is the Antithesis of Subject and Object

Mysticism is the inner state of consciousness whereby we escape from the isolated sphere of the soul to come into contact with the spiritual sense of being and divine reality. Mysticism resides in the depth and height of the spiritual life. It is intimate and hidden from the common view of most human beings. It is not a state of romantic subjectivism nor a dreamy condition of the soul. It is essentially realistic and is the catalyst that brings us into true freedom allowing us to surrender ourselves in prayerful oneness to the indwelling Trinity. Mystics seek to return God's perfect love especially through creative, loving works in God's world.

True mysticism presupposes mystery, viz., that which is inexhaustible and ineffable. It equally supposes the possibility of vital contact with this mystery and of a life in it and with it. Such a mystery is not a negative category, but is rather the positive fullness of life that is ultimately discovered by living in loving union with God.

Christian Mysticism

Christian mystics begin even before any well-developed mystical experience of God and the world with a faith-vision of the triune God as personal Creator. This triune God, Father,

Son and Holy Spirit indwell the Christian through the gift of divine grace. Primal grace is not a created "thing," but God's uncreated energies of love, living and operating in human persons to transform or divinize them into children of God. For such Christians, prayer is a gradual movement both inwardly and outwardly toward this Trinitarian presence throughout the universe. Such mystics discover above all the person, God the Father, begetting within the human soul the Son, Jesus Christ, who surrenders himself in total self-emptying back to the Father through his Spirit of Love personified.

The Journey Inward

Dag Hammarskjold writes in his diary:

The longest journey
Is the journey inward
Of him who has chosen his destiny
Who has started his quest
For the source of his being.[13]

But what a struggle it is to begin this long journey and so few human persons ever take the first steps. Carl Rogers describes the difficulty we human beings experience moving away from our "exterior" self to move toward the inner, true self:

Freedom to be oneself is a frighteningly responsible freedom, and an individual moves toward it cautiously, fearfully, and with almost no confidence at first.... They are in flux, and seem more content to continue this flowing current.[14]

There will always be the dilettantes who dabble in instant mysticism. They stay on the fringes of the inner desert, but they have the illusion of having gone into themselves. They have never left the flesh-pots of Egypt. They are still enslaved to their false ego.

There are, however, in all walks of life, true and sincere seekers of the truth. They yearn for authentic, inner freedom. They hunger to find their true self in the Absolute Other. They are ready to face death in order to find true life. "God, you are my God. I am seeking you. My soul is thirsting for you. My flesh is longing for you" (Ps 63:1). God can do anything with them for they have already seen that without God they have no true meaning. They are ready to let the masks and false idols come crashing down as they move deeper and deeper into the inner battle. Such persons courageously put the question to themselves at each moment of their lives and honestly wait for the answer to come back to them in silence: "Who am I, really?"

With Gabriel Marcel such a Christian "...has become once and for all a question for himself."[15] A stripping process occurs within the beginning mystics as they eagerly seek to stay "inside" themselves, groping for answers instead of running "outside" to be diverted from the important issue at stake. This sense of emptiness is the initial step toward a rich in-filling. They refuse to leave the battle but hold their ground as they continuously struggle in their heart to gain freedom from the pre-conditioning of their past involvements in a life of sense indulgence, emotional and intellectual blindness.

Such contemplatives stand stripped of any illusory self-power. Broken and sick, they confront God as the Divine Healer. They ride into the levels of inner darkness and death like Albrecht Durer's knight in his engraving, "Knight, Death and the Devil."[16] The knight is in full armor, riding through a valley accompanied by the figure Death on one side, the Devil on the other. Fearlessly, concentrating and with confidence he looks ahead. He is alone, but not lonely. In his solitude he seems to participate in a power which gives him courage to affirm him in spite of the presence of negatives of existence.

Alone with the Alone

Going into their heart contemplatives discover their incompleteness. Faith springs into being as they discover that they are not alone, but in the depths of their being lives the loving, creative presence of the indwelling Trinity. In their solitude they find communion. In their existential need for the transcendent God who alone can come to their rescue, they place all their hopes and aspirations. Poverty yields to a sharing in the riches of God's graces.

> But God, who is rich mercy, because of the great love he had for us, even when we were dead in our transgressions, brought us to life with Christ (by grace you have been saved), raised us up with him, and seated us with him in the heavens in Christ Jesus, that in the ages to come he might show the immeasurable riches of his grace in his kindness to us in Christ Jesus. (Eph 2:4-7)

Answering the Inner Call

God calls every individual human person to discover his/ her true self by responding to the exigencies of each moment. One great temptation in today's world of gimmicks and practical do-it-yourself gadgets is that we can discover and awaken to ever increasing intensity and authentic freedom our *inner self* by some quick method. Many of us might think: if we could only hit upon the right technique or find the suitable spiritual guide, we feel certain that this inner awakening would not only be facilitated, but would surely reach its fullness.

But this is to forget that the inner self is not a compartment of our being. It is characterized primarily by a spontaneity that necessitates our growth into greater personal freedom. Our inner self is engaged in a process of continued growth that involves our whole being. We cannot start with a static concept and deduce its essential properties along with various infallible means of bringing it to fruition. This is to ignore the existential reality of our inner self.

It is when you and I stand outside of our habitual, fragmented self that we experience ourselves as a *total Ego* or our true self on our deepest and highest level of existence as a person. It is our life, lived fully with all our potential, stretching forth with uncontained joy toward its spiritual fulfillment. Like a seed that has partially yielded to death and suddenly stretches forth to an unfolding, inner power commanding greater life, so our inner life awakens to a new awareness of a more total and unified existence. When it is stirred, it communicates a new life to our intelligence so that we reflectively and consciously live on a deeper level.

This awareness is not a thing we possess. It is a state of existence as sheer gift of God's grace whereby we *are*. It is a real, indefinable experience of new living relationships, of an *I* to God, to other human persons and to an energized world. This experience of the inner self disappears or pales into a shadowy replica of reality under the scrutiny of rationalization. It cannot be put into a conceptualized "box." It is not a "thing" and hence there is no trick, no method, no meditation that can cajole it out of its hiding. A disciplined asceticism can only bring about the proper climate in which the inner self may both be recognized and rendered more present. This climate produced by a spiritual regime includes such things as silence, poverty and detachment, purity of heart and passionate longing to surrender to God in every thought, word and deed (cf. 2 Cor 10:5).

God Is No Longer an External Object

Rudolf Otto has well expressed Meister Eckhart's teaching (†1327) that our end is to contemplate the Immanent God living within us and thus learn to adore and serve him indwelling immanently in all other human beings and throughout all of God's material creation:

> He only has God for whom God is no longer *objectum*, who lives God, or rather "is lived by God," borne up and impelled by the Spirit and the power of God. But the more this is realized, the more God as merely an object "disbecomes" from the sphere of his conceptions and thought, God becomes the inward power and the health of his spiritual life, so that in the "living waters" of righteousness and holiness, love is radiated, and the spirit itself goes forth passing to others and working the same effects in them. He has got rid of the conceived and apprehended God, because God has now become his inward power, by which he lives, but upon which he reflects less, the more completely and powerfully he lives in the Divine.[17]

Entering into Contemplative Prayer

One enters into a state of contemplation almost imperceptibly. After years of disciplined prayer in which we were principally the main *doers*, pondering words and scenes from Holy Scripture, making comparisons, drawing conclusions, we realize gradually that we enjoy simply resting in the presence of God. He is within and I am aware of his personal loving activity in my regard. I learn to let go. I breathe psychologically more deeply, more peacefully. I am discovering that I can with ease go down into my inner self and stretch out joyfully with my spiritual hands that seek to grasp God who now is more intimate to me than I am to myself, to quote St. Augustine's phrase.

I seem to have been given new, interior eyes that lovingly gaze on the indwelling Trinity. In that gaze I experience through faith, hope and love of the indwelling Holy Spirit how perfectly and infinitely God Trinity loves me. With new interior ears I ever so quietly listen to God as he communicates himself to me without words, images or any finite forms. It is no longer my praying with this or that faculty, now thinking this thought, now that. My whole being is immersed in God. My disparate activities seem suspended as I enter into a tranquillity that brings to me a sense of oneness with God.

My prayer now is not something I do so much as my entering into a state of being. *Enstasis,* a standing inside, best describes it. I seem to be standing inside my real self and no longer standing outside (*ekstasis*). I am now inside my deepest reality that brings with it a communion with God as I am standing also *in* him. I stand in his holy presence, loving him without words or images. Yet the totality of my being is in a tranquil state of loving surrender.

One of the perplexing features of this deeper prayer of the

heart is that the former ways which we used to measure our
"praying ability" now seem no longer to apply. In fact, because
such contemplatives are less actively engaged with their
imagination, understanding, will and affections, such can no
longer be used as an index of our prayerfulness. This is a state
of expanded consciousness brought about by an increased
infusion of faith, hope and love by the Holy Spirit.

It is only the Holy Spirit who assures us that we are united
with God and truly growing in greater loving union. It is also
the Holy Spirit who brings forth his gifts and fruits in our
loving relationships with other human persons. Our lives, now
rooted more deeply in the ultimate, reflect more exactly than at
any other earlier stage the worth of our prayer-life (Cf. Rm
8:26-27).

What we experience continually when the Spirit prays
within us is the utter conviction that we are God's beloved
children, loved infinitely by the Trinity from all eternity.
Where there is the Spirit there is liberty (2 Cor 3:18). The Spirit
breathes forth within our consciousness and unconscious (our
heart, as Scripture calls this union) through an infused
experience that now we *know* that God really loves us! "See
what love the Father has bestowed on us that we may be called
the children of God. Yet so we are!" (1 Jn 3:1).

It is through the power of Jesus Christ's Spirit that our
hidden selves are to grow strong, that Christ is to live in our
hearts through faith. Through the Spirit we are able to grasp the
breadth and length, the height and the depth of the love of
Christ. The Spirit will fill us with the "utter fullness of God"
(Eph 3:19).

Love and Freedom at the Core of Deeper Prayer

Love is the core and center of mysticism. God begins to reveal himself to the pilgrims who strip themselves from all attachments in order to be "recollected" or pulled together into a "still point" of continued attentiveness so that God might speak his Word made flesh, now risen and dwelling within us through his Spirit of love. Such higher knowledge and illumination cannot be achieved by our own efforts or by any limiting conceptual knowledge. Only an immediate, experiential knowledge given by God when he wishes and to whomever he wishes is the path to true contemplative knowledge.

It is the cloud of unknowing, the *"docta ignorantia."* It is the sole work of God given to the soul that he desires and this without respect to the merit of that individual person. Without this grace, no saint or angel can conceive of seeking it.

Praise and Thanksgiving

A true index as to the degree of our praying and how free we have become through the illumination and transfiguration of ourselves into our true selves in Christ is to be found in the quality and degree of our praise and thanksgiving that permeates our daily living. If we believe in God's dynamic, loving presence at each moment, we can only praise him for his love. We have new eyes to see each event in his uncreated energies of love. We soon by God's grace develop a new way of viewing all things, since our faith tells us that *all* things work unto good for those who love the Lord (Rm 8:28). With St. Paul we too can say through experience: "Be happy at all times; pray constantly; and for all things give thanks to God, because this is what God expects you to do in Christ Jesus" (1 Th 5:18).

We soon move into a spirit of constant adoration of God for his loving presence. His energizing love communicates itself in all things. Everything is a point of praising God, not only because of his gifts, but above all for his very own triune, loving presence. The distinction between what is painful, a setback, a calamity and what is pleasant, a success and honor, disappears as we see through all events and creatures that touch our lives as "signs" of God's great love for us.

This loving power is God's very own life, transforming the world into light and heat: the light that allows all of us to "see" God, loving us in each situation, and the heat to warm our human hearts to adore the almighty, tender loving God as we lovingly open ourselves to love one another. The love of God pours into us, allowing us to see the power of the Spirit of Jesus Christ working in the lives of all human beings, regardless of their culture or religion. We breathe more freely as we live on higher plateaus that stretch out into infinity. The walls and ghettoes that our fearful, anxious selves have constructed because we were living in darkness and ignorance and did not realize God was present in all things, these come crashing down.

We stretch out our empty hands and humbly ask God to fill them with his energies of love. We beg him to use our weaknesses in order that his glory, his *Shekinah,* may appear in each event. We cry out in pain that the full Christ be brought forth in glory in our world. We offer our hands and lips to be channels of the healing power of Jesus Christ among his people again. Praying incessantly is now, not so much saying prayers, but a living in constant consciousness of God's beauty, found "inside" of all matter.

We humbly take off our shoes, all our human securities, and in mute adoration we surrender to him in loving submission. Our obedience to God's will is the highest possible expression of our freedom as Jesus himself expressed utter freedom when he literally emptied himself, dying for love of us on the cross. God is at the heart of matter. And matter is moving, aided by our prayerful contemplation of God and our loving service of others, towards spirit. The world that is groaning under the limitations of matter is slowly emerging as a transfigured heavenly Jerusalem.

As we started this chapter on mysticism and freedom with the quote from Karl Rahner that the Christian of the future will have to be a mystic who has experienced Someone, or such a person will be nothing at all, I would like to conclude with another of his quotes as he strongly insists that only in deeper prayer can we enter into the Holy Spirit's gift of authentic freedom:

> No person can give him/herself the freedom needed
> to respond totally to God. For this task he needs to
> be set free by God himself, and he is set free only in
> prayer. Prayer then is the way, because it is the
> expression of human powerlessness, the affirmation
> of human fundamental nothingness and the cutting
> off of all means of escape.[18]

Chapter Eight

Freedom To Build a Better World

We have taken a journey on a search for the meaning of inner reality. We have called that search *mysticism,* the movement of a humble person on fire with love for God toward greater union with him. In the growing assimilation into God's very own life lies the consciousness of our unique personhood. The mystics who have experienced the personal love of God and are conscious that God accepts them, loves them, suffers for them even to the point of accepting death on the cross, can alone love others as all human beings should love. Such freed mystics realize that they have become fire and light. God, infinite love, loves with them. Their wisdom is to be one with the Trinity. This is love experienced that then begets love toward other beings, including the cosmos.

True mysticism is authenticated by the love that contemplatives show toward others in humble service. This alone, the acceptance of others in self-sacrificing love, proves that they have experienced a true love and freedom from the Source of all beauty and goodness. Any mysticism that does not reap a harvest in shared love toward others in the building of a better world according to God's eternal plan in the creative Logos, Jesus Christ, God-Man, is a deception and in the end is dehumanizing.

Thomas Merton summarizes the contemplatives'
relationships with the world and all its inhabitants:

> The world as pure object is something that is not
> there. It is not a reality outside us for which we
> exist.... The world has in fact no terms of its own...
> we and our world interpenetrate.... If anything, the
> world exists for us, and we exist for ourselves. It is
> only in assuming full responsibility for our world, for
> our lives and for ourselves that we can be said to live
> really for God.[1]

True mysticism is always begetting, becoming the other in
greater unity of love. As Christians advance in deeper prayer,
they begin to breathe the air of freedom that can come only as a
gift of the Holy Spirit. They learn their inner dignity to be the
gift of an eternal love act of God that always was and always will
be. They transcend time as they live in the *now* of God's
unchanging, holy love for them. As they experience deeply
God's abiding presence and his energizing love within them,
they learn how to give up all attachments to lesser desires and
loves in order to love only God Trinity and to find in the
Ultimate Source of all being all other loves.

Loving the Christ in Others

Part of this revelation by the Holy Spirit of our true
identity in God's eternal *now* love for us individually is also his
revelation that our neighbors and all other human beings
throughout the entire world have been made in that same image
and likeness to Jesus Christ. We begin to experience a facility to
turn to each person and love him or her through the Spirit's love
that abounds in our hearts (Rm 5:5). We contemplate others as

the saints and angels do — in God's eternal love made manifest in Christ Jesus.

Thus we can pierce through the false fronts that others live behind or that our own insecure false-self projects upon others. In direct and freely spontaneous love we give the love of God to all whom we meet. God is no longer an object far away or a vague concept. He is a triune community of love, a dynamic, creative force now loving and creating all of us and the whole world around us into "receptacles of God's goodness," in the words of St. Irenaeus. We know now that it is in a gentle receptivity to God's eternal, loving presence that we wait for him, resting in his all-pervading love.

And Yet, Not Yet!

And yet, we are still bound up in this bodily existence, joined to a world that groans together in travail, "....in one great act of giving birth" (Rm 8:22). The tension of experiencing our inner beauty and dignity as children of God through the Holy Spirit (Rm 8:15; Gal 4:6) and seeing by reflection our daily responses to that noble call and our true identity already realized in God's eternal gift of love fills us with a constant sense of humility and inner poverty. We cannot love others as we ought. Our reflection each day shows us how we have acted. We review in God the *not yet* situation and call out to him for greater healing.

From the Cross to Glory

As Jesus discovered his full and perfect freedom only in freely surrendering his whole life to the Father, so too we enter into our freedom as children of God as we abandon ourselves to the Father's love. But such surrender of ourselves to God's free will to do with us whatever he wishes means a constant readiness to die to our own self-controlled lives. This is the *cross* that Paul preached as a stumbling block to the Jews and the Gentiles (1 Cor 1:22-25).

We become free by contemplating the length and breadth, height and depth of the love of Jesus Christ (Eph 3:18). In every event, every thought, word and deed, we seek to witness to the freeing power of Jesus to take away all fear, loneliness, isolation and separation from the community of all other human beings.

The authentic test of the true, inner union with the indwelling Trinity must be measured by the degree that we love all others with a love that approximates more and more that which the Father has for us in his image, Jesus. "We have passed out of earth and into life, and of this we can be sure because we love our sisters and brothers" (1 Jn 3:14).

Ultimately true human as well as divine freedom consists in the ability to give oneself in love to all who approach us. As we experience in deep contemplation, in a continued dying-rising process from darkness to light, the presence of the loving, indwelling Trinity, the more we are impelled by the Spirit of God's love to go out and love others in a community of self-giving persons. Freedom is God's gift that enables us to experience our true uniqueness by the unity experienced when we die to our selfishness and love others for their own good.

We truly become free by rejecting the selfishness that enslaves us in order by contemplation to give ourselves freely to being the *slaves* of Jesus Christ. Only prayer, taught us by the Holy Spirit in the abandonment of the desert of our hearts, can lead us into such freedom. In Paul's words:

> You know that if you agree to serve and obey a master
> you become his slaves. You cannot be slaves of sin
> that leads to death and at the same time slaves of

obedience that leads to righteousness. You were once
slaves of sin, but thank God you submitted without
reservation to the creed you were taught. You may
have been freed from the slavery of sin, but only to
become "slaves" of righteousness. (Rm 6:16-18)

All is Loved in God and for God's Glory

As we are immersed in God Trinity and we find our
beautiful true self in the Trinity's perfect, infinite love for each
of us, so we open ourselves through the working of the Holy
Spirit to the Trinity working in all creatures. The same powerful
Trinity that radiates their mutual love for each other radiates
their uncreated energies within us and is found as the Source of
being for all other creatures. The world around us takes on a new
meaning and a new responsibility.

A transfiguring process takes place in our vision of the
world and of ourselves. The world has not changed. God's
active, loving presence was always there, but we were blinded to
his light. Now it seems as though the blind have been given full
sight. What lay in darkness before, now is suffused with the
radiance of God's transforming light. The poet, Gerard Manley
Hopkins, S.J., called it "contuition," a simultaneous awareness
of the individual nature and of the dynamic presence of God
Trinity as the ground of its being. The contemplative is
simultaneously aware of being created and intuitively sees his or
her relationship to the uncreative energies of God.

The early Greek Fathers called this contemplation of all
material creatures, *theoria physica*, the contemplation of the
Divine Logos in whom all things have their being (Jn 1:2). As
we move out of the exclusive realm of our own self-activity and
enter into the realm of God's immanent creativity in each

creature, God gives us, by the infusing of the Holy Spirit, the gift to see, in all creatures the *logoi*. The *logos* in each creature is its principle of harmony that underlies the relationship of this creature to God's all-embracing providence, and to God's comprehensive order of salvation.

Thus we begin to see that the whole world is interlocked and interrelated. Only such contemplatives enter into authentic freedom as they see the harmony existing among all creatures. They see the purpose, the raison d'être, behind every created being. Such freed contemplatives will never misuse these creatures for their own purposes, but they will always use them and work to develop them according to God's *logos*.

Called To Be Christ's Co-Creators

As true, Christian contemplatives intuitively perceive the created order as a continued outpouring of the Trinity's love, they ardently wish to become, with St. Paul, a reconciler of the whole universe through Christ back to the Father:

> And for anyone who is in Christ, there is a new creation; the old creation has gone, and now the new one is here. It is all God's work. It was God who reconciled us to himself through Christ and gave us the work of handing on this reconciliation.... So we are ambassadors for Christ. It is as though God were appealing through us, and the appeal that we make in Christ's name is: be reconciled to God. (2 Cor 5:17-21)

A new creation is seen coming forth by the power of Jesus Christ and his Spirit of love through our adoring cooperation. In Christ, God is incarnated and inserted into the groaning universe. He sustains each creature in its uniqueness and seeks to move each creature together with the whole created universe into its *pleroma* or fullness.

Such contemplatives begin to experience the presence of Christ everywhere, especially in other human beings. Christ is laughing in the joyful. He is suffering in the saddened. The more defaced the image of Christ in an individual, the more ardently does the contemplative wish to assist in re-creating it, so that Christ again shines forth with all his divine splendor latent in each person. We would wish with great responsibility to serve our neighbors with an active love that will smooth away lines of fear and grief and consternation on the face of humanity. We rejoice also when Jesus Christ, the eternal youth, conquers an individual's heart in order to bring forth in it joy and happiness.

To Sing the Praises of God

By our Baptism we are inserted into Christ as co-sharers of his role as Prophet and Priest. St. Peter writes: "But you are a chosen race, a royal priesthood, a consecrated nation, a people set apart to sing the praises of God, who called you out of the darkness into his own wonderful light" (1 P 2:9). St. John writes that if we love one another, it is because God lives in us, loving through us:

No one has ever seen God;
but as long as we love one another
God will live in us
and his love will be complete in us.
We can know that we are living in him
and he is living in us
because he lets us share his spirit.

...God is love
and anyone who lives in love lives in God,
and God lives in him. (1 Jn 4:12-16)

The Body of Christ: The Church

Through the Spirit of the risen Jesus, we Christians have been baptized into Christ's Body, the Church. We are now new creatures. A whole new world, like a leaven, has been inserted into the universe. This new creation is Christ the Head, joined to us, the members of his Body, the Church. Together we with Christ our Head are called in the freedom of the gift of the Spirit of love to reconcile the entire world and bring it into its fullness according to the eternal plan of the heavenly Father.

The Body of Christ, the redeemed humanity and the transfigured world brought about through our human cooperation with Jesus Christ, is in process of growing into its fullness. This is stated clearly in Vatican II's *Constitution on the Church in the Modern World:* "The Church, or in other words, the kingdom of Christ now present in mystery, grows visibly through the power of God in the world."[2] The mystical Christ has not yet attained to his full growth. He is to reach his fullness through all created activity that is under the direction of the Spirit of the risen Jesus.

Our human dignity consists in reaching our fulfillment by our freely working to bring about the salvation of the world. The more our every thought, word and deed is imbued with this transcendent and ultimate concern, the greater also will be our human growth, which is affected not only by our love for God and neighbor, but also by the measure of God's very own uncreated energies of love working in us and through us to fulfill his eternal plan.

This is not a Platonic, static plan, a universal idea in the mind of God that disregards our human intervention in free cooperation with him. We are to touch the immanence of God within all of matter and through our cooperative, synergistic labors with God's creative presence, we are to co-create this world with the Triune God.

God's Presence within Matter

A kind of Platonic dualism runs through much of Western Christian thought separating God from his material creation. We have placed God, spatially at least in our thinking and praying, *up there* and have forgotten the essential mystery of the Incarnation. God truly is available to us by being immanently *inside* of matter. We have already pointed out God's independent existence in all of his ineffable and incomprehensible essence. Yet he is always becoming present to his creatures by his "uncreated energies of love."

Before we can truly build a spirituality of work, we need to develop a spirituality based on the various modes of being in which the divine Persons of the Triune God are present to us. This will allow us to see God truly at the heart of matter, or better, it will allow us to discover the Trinity in the material world and in the activities that make up our daily existence.

Finding God Immanently in All Creatures

If our Christian faith tells us that the divine presence of God, like the rays of the sun, glows within the cosmos and that through our sensate life we make contact with this material world, why, then, do we seemingly fail to *see* God everywhere? Why can we not be in a constant attitude of worship, adoration and self-surrender to God in the midst of our daily work and our continued contact with the material world that surrounds us?

Our first step to be healed of our blindness and set free is to find God immanently present in all things. This sense of the divine immanence must begin first in prayer. We are a microcosm of the macrocosm. This immanent presence of God in us is the same immanence within all the material world, drawing all creatures into a unity in God.

The second step in a spirituality of Christian "worldliness" in the best incarnational sense is not merely to contemplate God in all things, but for us to surrender to God, who actively works to hold all things together (Ac 17:28). This step leads us to the third presence of God in matter where we discover God as energetic love. He is continuously, not merely present in all things, holding them in their being, but he is constantly creating the world. God is dynamically in motion as he creates the world through us human beings.

It is for us to recognize by deep faith that God is actively creating in all circumstances, be they our active works or simply events that happen to us as we actively accept them. "We know that by turning everything to their good, God cooperates with all those who love him, with all those whom he has called according to his purpose" (Rm 8:28).

The fourth step is to recognize by faith that God is a transforming, deifying, loving energy that is moving us and through us the entire material world into a oneness.

Matter Is Sacred and Diaphanous

The Kingdom of God is being fashioned by God and us human beings in a synergism to recapitulate all of creation into a harmonious unity. This is a process that the Greek Fathers called *theosis* or divinization. God is no longer merely the One on *High* or the *Within* of things. He is also the *Beyond*. We see ourselves at this stage of spiritual maturity as called by God to transform the earth in each creature and each atom. It is only at this stage of *insight* that Christians see a unity between the love of God and the particularity of each atom of the universe.

The following quote of Albert Einstein well describes this level of contemplation as the basis for true science in our modern world as well as true religion:

> The most beautiful and most profound emotion we can experience is the sensation of the mystical. It is the sower of all true science. He to whom this emotion is a stranger, who can no longer wonder and stand rapt in awe, is as good as dead. To know that what is impenetrable to us really exists, manifesting itself as the highest wisdom and the most radiant beauty which our dull faculties can comprehend only in their most primitive forms — this knowledge, this feeling is at the center of true religiousness.[3]

Matter is now sacred, as Pierre Teilhard de Chardin preached so effectively in his many writings. He states:

> Each one of our works, by its more or less remote or direct repercussion upon the spiritual world, contributes to perfect Christ in his mystical totality.[4]

The level of our freedom and contemplation of God's immanence in all the material world is measured by the faith vision that no longer distinguishes between two separated worlds, the sacred and the secular. Now for such Christians there is only the vision of the Body of Christ, still being formed from the material of this world through our cooperative and creative efforts under the guidance and power of the Holy Spirit of love. This is the fifth level of Christian consciousness that leads us to unite without inner strain and division "the passion of the earth and the passion of God."[5]

This summit guides and gives meaning to each new step along the way to a true mysticism of work and prayer. It is a sheer gift of God, given to those who seek to possess it and strive each day to grow in greater faith, purity of heart and fidelity to God's presences as we have outlined. I have tried to present this intuitive synthesis of the whole in a work I entitled: *The Cosmic Christ from Paul to Teilhard.*[6] This is a consciousness in one and the same act, of God and each creature in the world and their relationship. It is a penetrating act of *seeing* inside of the material world as it presents itself to our senses which allows us to go beyond the strict dualism that separates God and the world, work and prayer. Yet it does maintain the distinction that God is *not* the material world. The world truly becomes a *diaphany,* as Teilhard de Chardin so often describes it, of God's inner, active presence, to form the Body of Christ.

Called to Build the Body of Christ, the Church

As different members of the human body have varied functions, so, too, Christians have different and yet complementary vocations, pledging themselves in a variety of degrees of intensity to action, prayer or both together (Cf. 1 Cor 12:12-20). The material world has been called by God to achieve its fulfillment in the cosmic Christ, the risen Jesus who, as Lord, is Head of his Mystical Body and sanctifies human beings as his members. Through both the Head and the members the whole material world is to attain a place within the spiritualized Body

of Christ. The entire universe is to be recapitulated by the total
Christ and brought to completion to the heavenly Father.

All of Us Are To Help in Developing Creation

Any religious piety or prayer that does not answer God's
call to cooperate in building this entire world into a greater
union of love unto God's glory is enslaved to a false god and
not the God revealed by the Word of God made flesh. The
God-Man, in becoming the Head of the human race, is also the
Head of the entire material creation.

In such an incarnational vision of prayer and work,
whatever we add by way of our political involvements, art,
thought, technology, social, scientific and religious activities
can serve to bring the entire Christ to completion and to full
glory. Our greatest creative work consists in consciously
cooperating with the creative power of God according to the
mind of God to bring the universe into fulfillment. Thus true
Christian freedom is seen in our seeking always to live
according to the mind of God in all of our relationships. In this
way we contribute positively to the fulfillment of God's created
world. By remaining enslaved to our false self we fail to uproot
sinfulness first within ourselves and then in this world.

In such a vision of the distinction between the world and
God's sacred, immanent presence, the world and our
"worldly" occupations attain their fullness, by not becoming
changed into something sacred, but rather by becoming the
"place" or *locus* where human beings can meet God and bring
that segment of the material world into its fullness.

Through the Word made flesh and now, marvelously
inserted as sharer of God's eternal life into our material world,
we are the "branches" that extend his hypostatic union into our

historical time and material space. Edward Schillebeeckx,
O.P., well expresses this mystery:

> This also reveals the fact that thanks to Christ, all
> human history is swathed in God's love. It is
> assumed into the absolute and gratuitous presence of
> the mystery of God. The worldly and the temporal
> remain worldly and temporal; they are not
> sacralized, but sanctified by that presence, that is, by
> the God-centered life of Christ and of his faithful.[7]

Building the Body of Christ

As we turn within ourselves daily in prayer and purifying
reflection that heals us of our selfish love, we find Christ more
easily in our material concerns. We yield freely our talents to
his direction. We seek to live according to God's inner
harmony found in each event. We become his servants as we
lovingly work to serve others. It is possible by God's grace to
live and move and act out of a conscious love for God in the
most profane situations. Without detracting from our full
concentration on the given tasks at hand, our work can be the
very environment, a *divine milieu*, in which we adore and serve
God, who infinitely loves and serves us in Jesus Christ and his
Holy Spirit. This is the peak of true, Christian freedom.

God is calling us at every moment to work to build the
Body of his Son into its fullness. There can be no greater
humanizing force in our lives than to work consciously toward
this goal. We are continuously in process, through our daily
lives of activities and passivities, joys and sorrows, sin and
reconciliation, of being divinized into God's loving children by
becoming one in his only begotten Son.

As we know ourselves in the Father's eternal love, we

become the extension of his Son's Body, to bring others by our love, and God's love in us, into that Body.

A New Challenge to Christianity

In our modern world Christianity is being given a new challenge to join the forces of women and men of good will to salvage and reconstruct the world in which we live. The Church is being called back to its original mandate as handed down by the first Christian community in Jerusalem and taught by Jesus Christ, its Founder. The Spirit of the risen Jesus is already releasing a dynamism within the Church and among its leaders to carry out this mission.

No longer can Christians ignore the historical moment the entire world is now passing through. The Church, led by the initiative of our present Holy Father, is inviting such groups as the United Nations, the World Council of Churches and many other collective activist groups around the world to join in the reconstruction of a new world based on the dignity of each and every human being. The suffering people of the Third World are calling out to us to conscientize public opinion and to reorganize the world according to the universal principles of justice and freedom which are each person's human right.

The Church is an international organization, unique among such world structures. By Church we do not mean only the hierarchy or the ecclesiastical organization. The Church embraces all who believe in Jesus Christ and who commit their lives to the faith passed on through tradition and the sacraments. It turns to the world in which its members live to create a more just and peaceful society. It does so as its members hear and speak the living Word of God and organize themselves around a hierarchy to carry out what they have heard and experienced.

Pope Paul VI set the stage for the urgent responsibility to be assumed by the followers of Christ to create a better world in his important encyclical, *The Development of Peoples,* issued March 26, 1967. This followed two years after the close of the Second Vatican Council which outlined, especially in its *Pastoral Constitution on the Church in the Modern World* and its other decrees on Religious Freedom, Ecumenism and Relations with Non-Christian Religions, a renewed consciousness of the demands of the Gospel.

How beautifully and powerfully Pope Paul VI expressed this in his encyclical:

> Our charity for the poor in the world — and there are multitudes of them — must become more considerate, more active, more generous. To wage war on misery and to struggle against injustice is to promote, along with improved conditions, the human and spiritual progress of all human beings, and therefore the common good of humanity. Peace cannot be limited to a mere absence of war, the result of an ever precarious balance of forces. No, peace is something that is built up day after day, in the pursuit of an order intended by God, which implies a more perfect form of justice among all human beings.[8]

To Be a Freeing Power in Society

Jesus commissioned his first disciples to go forth and, not merely to announce the Good News about the coming of the Kingdom of God, but to bring his healing love and power to all mankind (Mk 16:16-18). Jesus continues to heal the broken ones of this world and to bring about a new age through those who surrender themselves to him and allow him to work through them to be a freeing power in their society.

Christians cannot leave the work of proclaiming the inbreaking of the Kingdom of God to the Church leaders. All are called through Baptism to be engaged in the liberation of the human race from all forms of slavery and affliction, spiritual, material and social. Wherever there exists any form of bondage, human indignity, injustice, hatred or oppression, the Kingdom of God suffers. Jesus came to set free all captives throughout the world — regardless of religion, color, nationality or culture.

The urgent issue that faces all people today is: how can we develop a society so as to ensure a more just and equitable distribution of necessary goods and services so that every human being may live on the physical, psychological and spiritual planes a life of human dignity befitting a child of God?

This requires that we put on the mind of Christ, who died for us all. By his Spirit of love working in us and among us, we can transform society, so that all human beings can in freedom choose to become more in the image and likeness of God. All human beings are called by God to such a task. But Christians, especially, through the revelation of God's love manifested in the love of his Son made flesh who died for all God's children in order to take away sin, selfishness and estrangement from each other, should strive to live in the unity of his Spirit by living in love and free service to each other, especially toward those in greatest need. Thus we show the world, not by arguments that God really exists, but we incarnate his love born again as we members live in Christ, our Head.

The Church now has its greatest opportunity to set in motion a universal revolution against those systems now exploiting the poor of this world and to positively to work for the transformation of the world as the only way to praise and worship the hidden God.

The words of Isaiah need to be put into action:

This, rather, is the sort of fast that pleases me... to
break unjust fetters and undo the thongs of the yoke,
to let the oppressed go and break every yoke, to
share your bread with the hungry, and shelter the
homeless poor, to clothe the man you see to be naked
and not turn from your own kind. (Is 58:6-7)

Loving God and Neighbor in Deed!

Christianity in this age of the Holy Spirit needs no armies
and fleets of ships to conquer the world for Christ. But by
being the spearhead for a liberation movement against strange
gods, it will be the prime, living example of what it means to
die to all worldly power that generates injustice, alienation,
ignorance and war. The Church will humbly go forth to be the
suffering servant of all those who are suffering from such
injustice and abuse of power.

Christians, by engaging in self-liberation, will call God
their Liberator and bring his freeing power to those imprisoned
by sinful social structures. They will speak of God to the world
through their actions promoting love and justice and peace.
God becomes real to a world only to the degree that his Word
is not only heard but eaten, and where those whom he sends
prophetically speak by actions done out of love, of the justice,
peace and freedom which are the heart of the Kingdom of God.

Epilogue

So much has been written about freedom. So much more will be written in the years to come as we strive in greater freedom to be our true selves in a society that often depersonalizes us. But these pages have been written to show that freedom is a gift from God. We, however, must cooperate in an ever ongoing process to be our true selves within the triune community of love. It is only we who can will to return to the freedom of the Father's house, to "indwell" again in God's loving presence and to serve him solely out of the sheer joy of being his children.

Yet even in this desire to be in our true home by being with the Father, we must see the gift of God's loving energies stirring us at the deepest level of our beings to want to become our true selves as God has always wanted us to be. This is a call to true contemplation. It is never given as God's gift in one static moment. It is a process that begins in this life, continues each moment of our earthly existence and accompanies us into the life to come as a continued growth in our uniqueness as persons freely loved by God the Father in Jesus Christ through the Holy Spirit.

Freedom is, then, actually the love of God Trinity working within us and around us throughout the entire universe in all God's creatures to impower us with a self-sacrificing love toward God and all of his creation. We become liberated as we exist on ever new levels of consciousness of our oneness with all in Christ. Freedom creates in us joy and the exciting desire to become ever more and more one with the whole universe as we experience a new capacity of being toward others, that enables us to receive *being* from their love returned.

Ultimately Heaven or the Kingdom of God is that state of inner freedom whereby we can allow the freedom of God's love to recreate us ever anew as his children and to send us out to actively love one another in his love. St. Paul assures us that "love does not come to an end" (1 Cor 13:8). We can conclude this book with the thought that freedom also never comes to an end. Freedom begets more freedom just as love begets more love. The Kingdom of God that is made up of God Trinity and their human children can best be described in the vision of St. John the Beloved Disciple:

> You see this city? Here God lives among human beings. He will make his home among them. They shall be his people, and he will be their God. His name is God-with-them. He will wipe away all tears from their eyes. There will be no more death and no more mourning or sadness.
>
> The world of the past has gone. Then the One sitting on the throne spoke: "Now I am making the whole of creation new," he said. "Write this: that what I am saying is sure and will come true."
>
> And then he said, "It is already done. I am the Alpha and Omega, the Beginning and the End. I will give water from the well of life free to anybody who is thirsty. It is the rightful inheritance of those who prove victorious and I will be their God and they will be daughters and sons to me." (Rv 21:3-7)

End-Notes

Introduction

1 F. Dostoevsky, *The Brothers Karamazov*, tr. Constance Garnett (London: Wm. Heinemann, 1912), pp. 268-269.

2 J. Breck, *The Power of the Word in the Worshipping Church* (Crestwood, NY: St. Vladimir's Seminary Press, 1986), p. 218.

3 Cf. The doctoral thesis, unpublished at the present, on iconography and psychotherapy (Pacific Institute: Carpenteria, CA, 1998) by Dr. Noel Plourde, *The Icon as Window to the Self*.

Chapter One: God's Freedom

1 Gustavo Gutierrez-Merino, *A Theology of Liberation*, tr. and ed. Sr. Caridad Inda and John Eagleson (Maryknoll, NY: Orbis Books, 1973), p. 27. Other leading writers on freedom and liberation, cf.: John Desrochers, *Christ the Liberator* (Bangalore, India: The Centre for Social Action, 1977); Juan Alfaro, *Esperanza cristiana y liberación del hombre* (Barcelona, 1972); B. Olivier, *Developement ou liberation* (Paris, 1973).

2 W. Brugger and K. Baker, *Philosophical Dictionary* (Spokane, WA: Gonzaga Univ. Press, 1972), p. 6.

3 M.J. Adler, *The Idea of Freedom* (Garden City, NY: Doubleday and Co., 1958), p. 616.

4 Cf. my book, *Gold, Frankincense and Myrrh* (NY: Crossroad Publishing Co., 1997), Ch. 3, *"Luminous Darkness: the Apophatic Way,"* pp. 45-55.

5 St. John Damascene, *De Fide Orthodoxa*, Bk. 50, no. 4; PG 94, 800 B.

6 N. Berdyaev, *The Beginning and the End*, tr. by R.M. French (NY: Harper Torchbooks, The Cloister Library, 1952), pp. 104 ff.; *Meaning of the Creative Act*, tr. by Donald A. Lowrie (NY: Harper and Bros., 1954), pp. 129 ff.

7 *Dream and Reality: An Essay in Autobiography*, tr. by Katharine Lampert (NY: Macmillan Co., 1950), p. 117.

8 N. Berdyaev, *Realm of Spirit and the Realm of Caesar*, tr. by D.A. Lowrie (London: Victor Gollaancz, Ltd., 1952).

9 Gregory Nazianzus, *Homilia XLH*, PG 36, 476.

10 Pseudo-Dionysius, *The Divine Names and the Mystical Theology*, tr. by C.E. Rolt (London: SPCK, 1920), *DN* 11,4, p. 69.

11 Cf. my book, *The Silence of Surrendering Love* (Staten Island, NY: Alba House, 1986), pp. 4-12.

12 Gabriel Marcel, *Metaphysical Journal*, tr. by Bernard Wall (Chicago: H. Regnery Co., 1952), pp. 26, 147, 221.

13 St. Gregory the Theologian, *Theological Orations* 3 (29), 3, PG 36; 77A. For a modern treatment of earth time, eternal and everlasting (in Greek, *aidion*), cf.: Georgios I. Mantzaridis, *Time and Man*, tr. from the Greek by Julian Vulliamy (South Canaan, PA: St. Tikhon's Seminary Press, 1996).

Chapter Two: Called To Be Free

1 Sergius Bulgakov, *"De Verbe Incarné"* in *La Sagesse Divine et la Théanthropie* (Paris, 1943), pp. 65-68.

2 Emil Brunner, *Man in Revolt* (London, 1953), pp. 97-98.

3 Karl Barth, *Church Dogmatics*, Vol. II, Part 2, p. 387 (Edinburgh: T. and T. Clark, 1961), tr. by A.T. Mackay et al.

4 See also Eph 1:9-11 and Heb 1:3.

5 St. Thomas Aquinas, *Summa Theologiae*, la 2ae, Q. 109, intro. 2nd ans. Q. 110, l ans.

6 Karl Rahner, *The Trinity*, tr. by Joseph Donceel (NY: Herder and Herder, 1970), p. 23.

7 K. Rahner, *Nature and Grace*, tr. by Dinah Wharton (London: Sheed and Ward, 1963), p. 24.

8 Cf. *Theological Dictionary of the New Testament (TDNT)* Vol. 2, Gerhard Kittell, ed., tr. by Geoffrey W. Bromiley, article by Heinrich Schlier, *"Eleutheria"*; pp. 487-502.

9 Nelson Glueck, *Hesed in the Bible*, tr. by A. Gottschalk (Cincinnati, OH: The Hebrew Union College Press, 1967) for an exposition of *aheb, hen, hanan* and *hesed.*

10 Cf. T.F. Torrance, *The Doctrine of Grace in the Apostolic Fathers* (Edinburgh: Oliver and Boyd, 1948).

11 Cf. Edmund J. Fortman, *The Theology of Man and Grace: Commentary* (Milwaukee, WI: The Bruce Publishing Co., 1966).

12 St. Basil, *Epistola* 234; PG XXX11; 869.

13 For future development of the divine energies, cf. my work, *Uncreated Energy* (Amity, NY: Amity House, 1987).

14 St. Irenaeus, *Adversus Haereses* (AH); Book V, 6; pp. 531-532, citation from *The Ante-Nicene Fathers*, Vol. 1, ed. by A. Roberts and J. Donaldson (Grand Rapids, MI: Eerdmans, 1962).

Chapter Three: Jesus — The Freest of All Human Beings

1 Malachi Martin, *Jesus Now* (NY: E.P. Dutton and Co., Inc., 1973), pp. 5-20.

2 Cf.: Jan Milic Lochman, *Reconciliation and Liberation*, tr. by David Lewis (Philadelphia, PA: Fortress Press, 1980); *Jesus Christ and Human Freedom*, Vol. 93, in series, *Concilium*, ed. E. Schillebeeckx and B. Van Iersel (NY: Herder and Herder, 1974), esp. articles by Leander Keck, *"The Son Who Creates Freedom,"* pp. 71-82; Rudolf Pesch, *"Jesus, A Free Man,"* pp. 56-70; John Desrochers, *Christ the Liberator* (Bangalore, India: The Centre for Social Action, 1977); Ernst Käsemann, *Jesus Means Freedom* (Philadelphia, PA: Fortress Press, 1970), tr. by Frank Clarke from the German.

3 Christian Duquoc, *Christologie, Essai Dogmatique, l'homme Jesus* (Paris: Cerf, 1969), p. 125.

4 Cf. also, Jn 5:30; 5:41; 7:28; 8:28; 8:50; Jn 14:24.

5 Cf.: R. Pesch, art. cit., pp. 66-67.

6 F. Malmberg, *Uber den Gottmenschen* (Frieburg, 1960), pp. 45-46, cited by Pesch, art. cit., p. 68.

7 G. Maloney, S.J., *Bright Darkness: Jesus-Lover of Mankind* (Denville, NJ: Dimension Books, 1977), p. 127.

Chapter Four: Broken and Enslaved

1   St. Augustine, *Confessions of St. Augustine*, Bk. 1, Ch. 1, p. 45, in Series, *Nicene and Post-Nicene Fathers*, ed. by Philip Schaff, Vol. 1 (Peabody, MA: Hendrickson Publishers, 1994).

2   Gabriel Marcel, *Problematic Man*, tr. Brian Thompson (NY: Herder and Herder, 1967), p. 53.

3   *Ibid.*, p. 100.

4   Rollo May, *Love and Will* (NY: Dell Publishing Co., Inc., 1969), p. 139.

5   Arthur Janov, *The Primal Scream* (NY: Dell Publishing Co., Inc., 1970), p. 25.

6   *Ibid.*

7   L. Triton, *The Magic of Space*, pp. 138-149, cited by Jon Mundy, *"On Fear,"* in *Spiritual Frontiers*, Vol. IV (Summer, 1972), no. 3, p. 171.

8   On the healing power of forgiveness see two recently published works: Sr. Martha Alkan, OP, *The Healing Power of Forgiving* (NY: Crossroad Publishing, 1997) and *Seventy Times Seven (The Power of Forgiveness)* by the Bruderhoff Community elder and author, Johann Christoph Arnold (Farmington, PA: Plough Publishing, 1997).

9   Dr. Gerald G. May, *Addiction and Grace* (San Francisco: Harper and Row, 1988), p. 14.

10 See my work, *Gold, Frankincense and Myrrh* (NY: Crossroad Publishing, 1997), pp. 107-108, 167.

11 G. May, p. 14.

12 St. John Cassian, *On the Holy Fathers of Sketis and on Discrimination* in *The Philokalia*, Vol. 1; ed. by G.E.H. Palmer, et al. (London: Faber and Faber, 1979), pp. 95-96.

13 Cf. Romano Guardini who well expresses this point in his work, *Freedom, Grace and Destiny* (NY: Pantheon Books, 1960), pp. 77ff.

14 G. May, p. 19.

Chapter Five: Jesus Sets Us Captives Free

1   Ernst Kasemann, *Jesus Means Freedom* (Philadelphia, PA: Fortress Press, 1970), tr. Frank Clarke from German, pp. 149-150.

2   Albert Camus, *The Fall* (NY: Vintage Books: Random House, 1956), tr. Justin O'Brien, p. 118.

3   Cf. Peter Richardson's excellent work, *Paul's Ethic of Freedom* (Philadelphia, PA: Westminster Press, 1979).

4   See my work, *The Mystery of Christ in You: The Mystical Vision of Saint Paul* (Staten Island, NY: Alba House, 1998), pp. 21-33.

5   George Montague, *The Living Thought of St. Paul* (Milwaukee: The Bruce Publishing Co., 1966), p. 143.

6   Cf. Leander Keck, *"The Son Who Creates Freedom"* in *Jesus Christ and Human Freedom*, op. cit., p. 74.

7   Cf. N. Berdyaev, *Freedom and the Spirit*, op. cit., pp. 117-157. It is difficult to know who influenced whom, but Tillich's presentation is the more complete and penetrating. See also, Arturo Paoli, *Freedom To Be Free*, tr. Charles Underhill Quinn (Maryknoll, NY: Orbis Books, 1973), especially Ch. 2: pp. 15-26.

[8] P. Tillich, *The Interpretation of History* (NY: Charles Scribner's Sons, 1936), p. 26.

[9] Tillich, *The Protestant Era* (Chicago: Univ. of Chicago Press, Abridged edition, 1957), p. 57.

[10] Tillich, *Theology of Culture* (NY: Oxford Univ. Press, 1959), p. 7.

Chapter Six: The Freeing Power of the Spirit

[1] N. Berdyaev, *Slavery and Freedom*, tr. from the Russian by R.M. French (London: Geoffrey Bles: The Century Press, 1943) pp. 252-254.

[2] For a thorough presentation of the concept of *spirit* in both the Old and New Testaments, cf. John L. McKenzie, *Dictionary of the Bible* (Milwaukee: Bruce Publishing Co., 1965), pp. 840-845.

[3] Cf. Hendrikus Berkhof, *The Doctrine of the Holy Spirit* (Richmond, VA: John Knox Press, 1964), p. 26.

[4] *Ibid.*, p. 27.

[5] See my work, *Man — the Divine Icon* (Pecos, NM: Dove Publications, 1973).

[6] St. Irenaeus, *Adversus Haereses*, Bk. V, Ch. 6, 1, in *The Ante Nicene Fathers*, Vol. 1, ed. A. Roberts and J. Donaldson (Grand Rapids, MI: Eerdmans), pp. 531-532.

Chapter Seven: Mysticism and Freedom

[1] Karl Rahner, *Theological Investigations*, Vol. VII (NY: Seabury, 1971), p. 15.

[2] M.C. Richards, *The Crossing Point* (NY: 1978), p. 5.

[3] G.M. Hopkins, *"Hurrahing in Harvest"* in *A Hopkins Reader*, ed. John Pick (NY/London: Oxford Univ. Press, 1953), p. 15.

[4] Anthony Haglof, O.C.D., *"Psychology — Contemplation and the East"* in *Spiritual Life* (Fall, 1975), p. 155.

[5] Cf. my work, *Prayer of the Heart* (Notre Dame, IN: Ave Maria Press, 1981).

[6] Ann and Barry Ulanov, *Religion and the Unconscious* (Philadelphia, PA: Westminster Press, 1975), p. 13.

[7] Dr. Ira Progoff, *The Symbolic and the Real* (NY: McGraw-Hill Book Co., 1963), pp. 69-75.

[8] Jung, *Two Essays in Analytical Psychology* in *Collected Works*, Vol. 7 (Princeton, NJ: Princeton Univ. Prsss, 1969), p. 183.

[9] A. Deikman, *"Experimental Meditation"* in *The Highest State of Consciousness*, ed. John White (Garden City, NY: Doubleday Anchor, 1972), pp. 203-223, and *"Deautomatization and the Mystic Experience"* in *ibid.*, pp. 25-46.

[10] Cf. Deikinan's, *"The Meaning of Everything,"* unpublished ms. (Boulder: University of Colorado Medical School, 1970).

[11] Bernard Lonergan, S.J., *Method in Theology* (NY: Seabury Press, 1972), pp. 6-13.

[12] Roberto Assagioli, *Psychosynthesis* (NY: Viking Press, 1971), p. 17.

[13] Dag Hammarskjold, *Markings*, tr. Leif Sjoberg and W.H. Auden (London: Faber and Faber, 1964), p. 58.

[14] C. Rogers, *On Becoming a Person* (Boston: Houghton Mifflin Co., 1961), p. 171.

[15] G. Marcel, *Problematic Man*, tr. Brian Thompson (NY: Herder and Herder, 1967), p. 55.

[16] P. Tillich uses this example in his *The Courage to Be* (New Haven, CT: Yale Univ. Press, 1952).

[17] Rudolf Otto, *Mysticism East and West,* tr. B. Bracey and R. Payne (NY: Oxford Press, 1932), pp. 150-151.

[18] Karl Rahner, *On Prayer* (NY: Sheed and Ward, 1968), p. 15.

Chapter Eight: Freedom To Build a Better World

[1] T. Merton, *Contemplation in a World of Action* (Garden City, NY: Doubleday, 1971), p. 54.

[2] *The Church in the Modern World* in *The Documents of Vatican II,* ed. Walter M. Abbott, S.J. (NY: America Press, 1966); Ch. III: #39; pp. 237-238.

[3] Quoted by Lincoln Barnett, *The Universe and Dr. Einstein* (NY: New American Library, 1962).

[4] Teilhard de Chardin, *The Divine Milieu* (NY: Harper and Bros., 1960), ed. Bernard Wall, p. 31.

[5] Pierre Cren, *"The Christian and the World according to Teilhard de Chardin"* in *Concilium* , Vol. XIX (Paramus, NJ: Sheed and Ward, 1966), p. 42.

[6] G.A. Maloney, S.J., *The Cosmic Christ from Paul to Teilhard* (NY: Sheed and Ward, 1968).

[7] E. Schillebeeckx, ed., *"The Church and Mankind"* in *Concilium,* Vol. I (NY: Paulist Press, 1964), pp. 81-82.

[8] Pope Paul VI: Encyclical, *The Development of Peoples (Populorum Progressio),* March 26, 1967, no. 76.

ST PAULS

This book was designed and published by St. Pauls/
Alba House, the publishing arm of the Society of St.
Paul, an international religious congregation of priests
and brothers dedicated to serving the Church through
the communications media. For information regarding
this and associated ministries of the Pauline Family of
Congregations, write to the Vocation Director, Society
of St. Paul, 7050 Pinehurst, Dearborn, Michigan 48126.
Phone (313) 582-3798 or check our internet site,
www.albahouse.org